GETTING ISH DONE

5 SECRETS TO STOP PROCRASTINATING & GET MORE DONE IN LESS TIME!

GETTING ISH DONE
-5 Ways to Stop Procrastinating and Get More Done in Less Time!
Copyright © 2024 by Charles Bond. All rights reserved.
No part of this publication may be reproduced, stored in a retrieval system, or transmitted in any way by any means – electronic, mechanical, photocopy, recording, or otherwise – without the prior permissions of the copyright holder, except as provided by USA copyright law.
The author or publisher assumes no responsibility for errors or omissions. Neither is liability assumed for damages resulting from the use of information contained herein.
Unless otherwise indicated, scripture quotations are taken from the King James Version of the Bible. Copyright © 1979, 1980, 1982 by Thomas Nelson, Inc. All Rights reserved.

FIRST EDITION
Published in 2024
The Philemon Project LLC
2200 Olive St., Kansas City MO,64127
www.CharlesBond.com

Written by: Charles Bond | therealcharlesbond@gmail.com
ISBN: 978-0-9860732-3-6

Library of Congress Case
Bond, Charles
GETTING ISH DONE -5 Ways to Stop Procrastinating and Get More Done in Less Time!
Case Number 1-13456083661 | January, 2024

Library of Congress Cataloging-in-Publication Data
Category: Christian Living, Motivational & Inspirational
Cover Design by: Christopher Lewis
Format & prep for publishing by: Eli & Jahshua Blyden | EliTheBookGuy.com
Published & Printed in the United States of America | Tampa, Florida

Foreword

You might be surprised at what happens to be the biggest nation in all the world. The answer is not Canada, China, Russia, or America. All of those are indeed large countries, but they are not the largest nation. I strongly believe that the biggest nation in the entire world is procrastination!

Every day, throughout the world, in all walks of life there are countless people who are plagued by procrastination when it comes to their personal and professional pursuits. My definition of procrastination is: Putting off for tomorrow, what could be done today. The good news is there's a resource available to help individuals overcome the afore-mentioned problem.

Bishop Charles Bond's new book, "Getting Ish Done," is a must-read book for anyone desiring to filibuster less and be more productive. These pages of this writing are filled with strategies that will help readers to better manage their time and schedule. Applying the principles from each of these five chapters, will provide to be very profitable in many ways. Let your journey begin now and start Getting Your Ish Done!

– Dr. Kerwin B. Lee
Senior Pastor of Berean Christian Church
Stone Mountain, Georgia

Getting ISH Done

The Making of
Charles Edward Bond Jr.

This Book is dedicated to every Pastor, preacher, person, pupil, and participant who has had an impact, influence, and made an investment in this force of nature named Charles Edward Bond Jr.
I call it the making of Charles Edward Bond Jr.

CHARLES E. BOND SR. (posthumously) AND SHIRLEY BOND the best parents on the planet.MY SIBLINGS McKinley Britton "Punch" (posthumously)(Venus), Anthony Britton (posthumously), Jerry (you're not just my brother-in-law you are my Brother) Sharon Williams, Gwendolyn Clark, Brendolyn Bond (Baby sister), The Amazing Members of The Mt. Pleasant M.B. Church of Kansas City Missouri, Dr. Frank E. Ray Sr. (my Rabbi) and the New Salem Baptist Church of Memphis. Pastor Donald Johnson and the Oak Grove Church, My former beloved Work wives, Mary Smith and the illustrious ROSE FIELDS, Pastor Ephen Melton (a man who believed in me when I dint even believe in myself) Pastor Mark Davis, Pastor Delvekio Wilson my bestie better known as LD) and your lovely wife Sand, Beverly Patrick, my favorite Actresses Ms. Cicely Tyson (posthumously) Lupita , Taraji , Chiwetel Ejiofor, Denzel Washington Brad Pitt, Oprah Winfrey, Dr. J. G. McCann (posthumously) and the Rabbi Dr. G.L. Dickson , Rivers Glover the 1st and Dr. Ken Campbell the Dr. Brothers in my Texas Connection, Rabbi Jasper W. Williams 3rd and Pastor Alecia Williams (yes I am still the 1st Friend) (my conscience) Apostle Ricky Floyd and Sheila Floyd (Pretty Ricky what would my life be without you bruh), Dr. Darrell Harrington and the

Harrington crew over at New Sardis, Juliet H. in St. Louis , Dr. Nathan Nevell Nance, Bishop Dale Bronner, The Late Bishop Willie James Ellis and Mother Beverly Ellis (posthumously) , Percy and Elaine Winn (Laine make sure he calls me before Saturdays PLEASE) , Greg Paige who was my college buddy and introduced me to The first church I was privileged to serve as pastor the Samuel Chapel M.B. Church of Ashland Ms., Dr. John Crittle (Every Preacher needs a you in their life). Dr. C. DEXTER and Shirley WISE, Pastor Donald Slack and Connie (Your brotherhood is unmatched, and you are a game changer in your words you are good for me sir), Samuel Chapel Missionary Baptist Church Ashland Mississippi, Jeffrie Chapel M.B. Church Abbeville Mississippi, Travelers Rest M.B. Church Columbus, Ohio. New Wine Church International Columbus Ohio, and Memphis Locations. The awesome members of The Mt. Pleasant M.B. Church in Kansas City Missouri, Laneen A. Haniah (Dr. Intimacy). Pastor Marvin Chapman (I need 250 out of ya today rev), Bishop Rosie O'Neal (meeting you changed everything) Uncle Tellis Chapman. Brother Charles Robinson in Ohio (you've been my Barnabus). Dr. John and Lady Adolph, My Uncle Bishop Edgar and (te te) Sheila Vann (God used you both to reset my belief in myself). Pastor Kenny and lady p Turner (bruh you still owe me for putting that dent in the white escalade), My predecessor Pastor Louis Henderson Bell Jr and Lady Ethel M-Like Bell (my Grand pastor and Glama), Elliott "poison" Ivey Sr., the one and only Marty Peters (what can I say about you two), Dr. Jothany Blackwood (my rider) Minister A.J. (art) and Malinda Williams (taught me a major Lesson from my losses). The Memphis mafia, minister alliance Dr. Gerald Rayborn, my Cousin Pastor Carl E. Shields and Mrs. Frankie, Leroy James (hen), my brother Pastor Clinton McFarland (you put me on, and I'll never forget you), Dr. Jamal Bryant, you guided us through a whole Pandemic without even knowing it, Bruh. The late NATHANIEL COOPER, My sister CUZN LATARSHA MCCRAY, Dr. Ralph D. West Sr Story time broke my shell of shame, Dr. J. L.

Payne (posthumously), Sheila Taylor, Bishop Edward and lady Beverly Stephens (Bishop I'm keeping you as cuz and Bev has been emancipated out of the family, Pastor Deldrick and Sharon Leasure (the most unselfish First family I've ever met), Dr. Q. Respress, Harry and Elizabeth Scot (posthumously). My Bestie and BFF Kristen Elizabeth Yates (The KEY), Pastor Lamont B. Monford Sr.

Special thanks to Mrs. Maryellen and my A and A printing family. You guys and gals always get me done! Berneka McDonald you stepped in stepped up and showed out but Don't WORR I gotcha!

Ms. Alisha Tuff Hill One the most Game Changing Queen Slaydometrist's I've -ever met I LOVE YOU.

Getting ISH Done

Preface

The Beginning of Wisdom is To Call a Thing by Its Correct Name!
~Chinese Proverb

No Table of Contents, fancy heartfelt thank you lists, long forwards, or repetitive prefaces needed. I'm going to jump right in, feet first.

Why am I doing this book in a non-traditional manner and not following the literary rules, or normal examples, and models, you might ask? Because I don't waste time with things or people who are a waste of my time. Secondly, you've purchased this course and my book because you have a burning desire to get your Ish DONE; and the last thing you need is a bunch of useless space filler information from another author and stranger.

I will at least give you my why to my approach. In 2021 while we were all dealing with the throes of a Global Pandemic covid-19, I went through a series of 3 major losses. My oldest and only living brother died in February of that year. In June I went through a painful divorce from a woman whom I still love dearly. And to make matters worse my church and I were hosting a national conference, called Next Steps: Transforming the church culture to minister in a post pandemic paradigm. Although I'm a leader, I was not about to act like I had all the answers to help the local church that I was called to lead, nor the universal church, which I still believe is the bride and body of Christ (Flaws and all), began to rebound, rethink, and reshape how we do ministry. Although I did not have the answers, I had relationships with Leaders and global influencers who were already turning the corner and actively doing post pandemic style ministry, so we brought them to Kansas City Missouri to show us in our region, innovative techniques, and practices that their churches and congregations were using to lead beyond the crisis, and calamity of Covid-19. Having said that, seven months after my brother transitioned (and we had to say goodbye over an iPad thanks to my niece who was able to get into the hospital being a powerful medical professional that she is, because most hospitals had a no visitation rule in effect. The final blow was on October 27th, 2021, my father for whom I'm named went home to be with the Lord. I found myself in November of 2021 at the same cemetery burying my father, man what a year. The point of me sharing these facts is to let you know the most important lesson that I learned out of this period. That despite grieving 3 losses and major life changes, my Ish never stopped. In other words, I still had to get Ish done. The main lesson that I regurgitate as often as there is a hearer to hear; is this:

It is Arrogant to assume God owes us more time.

I am not saying don't look positively with hope to the future. I am not saying that we should live our lives with fear and trepidation of uncertainty. Neither am I saying we should not plan. And I am certainly not saying that we should ever live our lives in fear of death. I am simply sharing that my convictions of reflections over the period and events that took place in this season of my life led me to the revelation that we arrogantly assume that there will be more time to keep delaying, putting off or getting around to things, when the truth is all, we have is right now. As the adage goes _**yesterday is history, tomorrow is a mystery, yesterday is in the tomb, and tomorrow is in the womb; all we have is right NOW!**_

Please do not think that I'm a person who drives with one foot on the gas and the other foot on the brakes. However, I am a person who walks each day with urgency, not pressure of knowing fully that while I have breath in my body, we are privileged to be standing on the ground and the ground is not standing on us. That's God's gift that's why they call it the present and how we treat gifts determines in the future rather or not we will receive more.

Therefore, I walk with authority and humility, being grateful for every moment that God gives me. Yet I do my best to be a great steward of the time I've been allotted, for time is the only commodity we can't recycle. We should not handle it pridefully, but rather preciously and reverently with the spirit of gratitude. As I often say:

Never let getting ahead Go to your Head.

The truth is that you and I both have been assigned a certain amount of ISH to get done in our lives, so let's get to it. The main thing between you and your ISH (which only you can define) is a thing called: PROCRASTINATION. Now let's define the word.

Procrastinate verb pro·cras·ti·nate prə-ˈkra-stə-ˌnāt prō- procrastinated, procrastinating. Synonyms of procrastinate transitive verb.

: to put off intentionally and habitually intransitive verb: to put off intentionally the doing of something that should be done.

procrastinate: it comes from the Latin prefix pro-, meaning "forward," and crastinus, "of tomorrow." The word means moving or acting slowly so as to fall behind, and it implies blameworthy delay especially through laziness, apathy or lack of enthusiasm.

Some define procrastination as the act of delaying or putting off tasks until the last minute, or past their deadline. Some researchers define procrastination as a form of self-regulation failure characterized by the irrational delay of task despite potentially negative consequences.

So, when I look at the textbook definition of the word procrastinate there are several words that keep standing out and they are the words act, do and to. Simply meaning that procrastination is due to a decision not do something, that in turn could have consequential effects on your future self. Basically, choosing to not do your Ish for whatever reason. Now without discounting the fact that life happens to all of us. as I afore mentioned, death and divorce happened to me. Yet my bills and responsibilities, obligations etc. did not cease due to my circumstances. Yet the reason I approach this topic with both grit and grace is because I used to be a procrastinator. Whether it was putting off exercise, starting an important task, schoolwork, you name it, I was the master at it. As a result, I became a poster child for a sign that I once read on a marquee years ago that said:

If it wasn't for the last minute nothing would get done.

It was after I saw the toll that it was taking on my life, my income as well as my health that I had to make a change. It was through becoming manically, uber, and intentionally focused that I began to develop the reputation as a doer, and no longer a delayer. Thus, people started saying Charles you always get Ish done.

As I stated in the opening of this section that the beginning of wisdom is to call a thing by its correct name. Please note that Ish, although it is a common colloquialism of the hour in which we live, can only be defined by you. Out of nearly 8 billion people in the world, you have come across my book and course on getting Ish done which tells me that you can identify with the fact and admit that I am not the only one that would catch the occasional case of what I call stuck-i-tis and get frozen in overthinking, or get overwhelmed with the list of tasks staring you in the face.

Well fear no more you are about to embark on becoming an accomplishment guru. Let me be ridiculously clear. My book and E-course are about more than how to get the boxes checked off your to do list, but rather it is about tapping into your inner winner so that you can reach your destiny and turn your dreams into reality. I once read a quote that said the best way to predict the future is to create it. And I will admit that's what you are on the cusp of in this present moment. I will give you the tools and techniques along with the wisdom that I have learned and gleaned over the years from some of the world's greatest teachers, gurus, and top influencers who've mastered major achievements and global exploits. I will not be surface but rather get to the bare-knuckle steps necessary to get your Ish done.

WHAT IN THE ISH IS GOING ON HERE?

Hello, welcome to the first day of the next phase of your life. My name is Charles Bond, better known as Mr. getting Ish done. I've spent the last three decades establishing myself in the space of assisting others in carrying out and completing their assignments. In other words, getting their Ish done. I'm not going to waste precious time touting my resume or wagging my own tail. I just want to lay the foundation of our time together on the fact that as an authority in this space I pride myself in being ***check-a-out-able***. It's a word I coined because if you are like me and have seen a thing or two, you already know that there are plenty of illusionists out there, I'm just not one of them. Now prepare to take copious notes and let's begin the journey to get you from concept to completion by applying the principles and action steps that are proven.

Let's start with a working definition of Ish. Because again only you can define what your Ish is.

Ish is an acronym that stands for:
I - intentional
S - strategic
H - habits

And each letter points to the action steps necessary to make your Ish a reality.

The **I is for intentionality** the bases for your launching pad which is focus.

in·ten·tion·al (adjective) - done on purpose; deliberate:

SIMILAR: deliberate, calculated, conscious, intended, planned, meant, considered, studied, knowing are words that are synonymous with intentionality.

You must be willing to invest in your focus or you will never finish or accomplish much that's worthwhile. Intentionality is when you invest in the tools or knowledge that will get you to your desired result expeditiously.

I call this investment which means to (in)(internal, inward, inside) (vest) which derives from the French word vestments or to dress or clothes. This means investing is an inside job. You must dress inwardly before you dress outwardly. What good would it be to have Gucci, or Prada on your body but your soul inside is naked? What good is it to have Christin Louboutin (red bottom) shoes on your feet and your soul is barefoot? What good would it be for you to eat porter house steaks or the finest of foods known to man and your soul is malnourished. My point is success, salvation, and such are more about what you have in than what you have on. The first step in getting your Ish done requires, and demands investing in oneself. Investing in coaching, seminars, books, wisdom, and the tools necessary to assist you in seeing your Ish through. That's how I know you are almost there, because just by purchasing this book you've already proven you are willing to invest in you. I will deal more in depth on this subject matter in upcoming chapters.

The **S is for strategic**. My friend, there's an adage that says, if you fail to plan you plan to fail; and this unfortunately is only part true. You must have a plan, but also a strategy or strategies. It is of utter most importance to plan and be strategic because plans change, plans can be altered, due to unforeseen circumstances and may require you to pivot. However, if you have strategies there's no need to panic because at best you still can control your controllables. Remember this:

A VISION WITHOUT A STRATEGY IS A CURSE

Theres nothing more frustrating than seeing where you want to go, but not having a clear-cut path on how to get there. The s also means that you:

S - stop self-diagnosing, stop using old keys attempting to open new doors and sow where you want to go because seeds stop cycles. Every woman is familiar with a monthly cycle, the only way to offset or stop the cycle is to put a seed there. Plans are the vision, whercas strategy is the mission statement of how we achieve and arrive at the vision. Strategies are like the smart goals assessment you read about in leadership books and seminars. If you ever have attended a mastermind, or leadership conference especially in corporate American companies want to know if the people they have in charge of running their corporations and operations have smart goals. Smart goals are.

Specific: Increase the chances that you're able to accomplish your business goals by making sure they're well-defined. Determine who, what, where when and why.

Measurable: Develop criteria for measuring progress toward your business goals. Detail the key indicators that help you decide if you reach your goal by quantifying them.

Achievable: Create goals for your business that are attainable and achievable by ensuring that you and your team have the skills and resources needed to reach the goal.

Relevant: Align your company's goals with the overall objectives of your business and the realities of the market.

Time-based: Give yourself and your staff a deadline for reaching your goal to provide a sense of urgency and the opportunity to schedule the steps needed to achieve the goal.

All of this is connected to your strategy.

Lastly the **H is for habits**. To become a person who no longer allows procrastination to delay your dreams and derail your destiny, you must have healthy habits. One great philosopher said that the keys to your success are hidden in your daily routine. You see habits are behaviors you have developed through repetition. I wrote a quote once that said, *"I cannot hear what you are saying because your actions are screaming so loud."* My friend, your ways tell me more about you than your words. We will put into practice some habits that if you are willing to abide by the process you will be getting more Ish done in less time.

Now allow me to lay all my cards on the table. I teach biblical principles that can be applied in business or one's personal life to achieve all that God has assigned for you to do while here on earth. I am not attempting to convert you however I need to be ridiculously clear that the foundations of my teachings are all biblical. And I only state this because personally I believe integrity is key to partnership. The principles I teach also rest upon one main axiom. If you practice the principles, you will possess the promises. The bible is a book of promises; however, every promise is proceeded by a principle.

The H also stands for honor as well as having the ability to both heed and hear wisdom.

Before we move on, I want to be ridiculously clear that YOU AND ONLY YOU CAN DEFINE WHAT YOUR ISH IS.

YOUR ISH WON'T DO IT SELF!

I learned many years ago when I started writing books that understanding things at its least point of sensibility is key to fueling the why behind a thing making sense. In other words, for me breaking down why procrastination had ruled my life before the shift was tantamount to my cracking the code. One of my teachers said it best *THE SOLUTION IS INSIDE THE POLLUTION, BASICALLY THE ANSWER IS INSIDE OF THE PROBLEM.* What Aggravates you is a cue to what you've been assigned to change or effect! Here is a quotable tweet for you **"some stuff will never happen to you until you first learn how to happen to it".** I remember once a facilitator said two lifechanging and game changing statements during their presentation that were eye opening. They first stated, "BOOKS DON'T WRITE THEMSELVES" and then went further to quantify their previous statement by saying that they hated to hear people say to potential authors that there is a book inside of them. The truth is there is no book inside of anyone. There are unorganized thoughts and ideas inside of us that require the discipline of sitting down and typing out the book. Now of course this was pre-AI era, but nonetheless the statement was true. Because books don't write themselves. And the reality for you, my friend, is your Ish won't do itself.

Bare knuckle fact- your Ish can out stare you. in other words, your Ish will be right there staring you in the face until you get it done. I remember talking about writing books; however, my excuse was that I didn't take typing in high school. Excuses Excuses Excuses. One day I read something that was sobering.

The size of the Giant in front of you is a sign of the David inside of YOU!

Until David faced the giant Goliath, every day the bible says that Goliath would come out and mock the armies of Israel.

1 Samuel 17:4 (TLB)
⁴ Then Goliath, a Philistine champion from Gath, came out of the Philistine ranks to face the forces of Israel. He was a giant of a man, measuring over nine feet tall!

1 Samuel 17:48-51 (TLB)
⁴⁸ As Goliath approached, David ran out to meet him and,
⁴⁹ reaching into his shepherd's bag, took out a stone, hurled it from his sling, and hit the Philistine in the forehead. The stone sank in, and the man fell on his face to the ground.
⁵⁰ So David conquered the Philistine giant with a sling and a stone. Since he had no sword,
⁵¹ he ran over and pulled Goliath's from its sheath and killed him with it, and then cut off his head. When the Philistines saw that their champion was dead, they turned and ran.

Without printing the whole passage, I encourage you to go read the whole chapter of 1ˢᵗ Samuel chapter 17. Yet the gist of this Old Testament narrative is that David did not wait to act, nor did he cower in fear at pending danger. He took the bull by the horns approach, even when others around him didn't have full confidence in his abilities. This giant was taunting day and night the army of Saul, and everyone was afraid to face the giant. However, David on a care package delivery mission to his brothers who were in the army, overheard there was a reward for whomever could defeat the giant. This giant would agitate and aggravate the Israeli army day and night and one version says that the army of Saul was sore afraid. Here's a clue to what ISH you should also be doing. What aggravates and agitates us is also a sign of what we have been assigned to fix, address, remedy, or change. I've personally discovered that one of the things that agitates me and aggravates me the most is seeing people who have potential, purpose, passion, and a plan, but allow procrastination to stall their dreams.

Ladies and gentlemen, nothing aggravates me more than seeing people sit, and sleeping on themselves when I know that they have Ish to do!

Thus, I decided to write the book I would want to read, Getting Ish Done: 5 Secrets to stop procrastinating and get more done in less time.

It is a road map to the life that you not only desire to live but have been designed and destined to live while here on planet earth. As we proceed this is not another self-help guide. This book is not the manifesto of accomplishing thing's advice one size fits all answer. This is a tool for the practices needed to get your Ish Done. So, stop thinking about it, stop dreaming about stop wishing for it and not let's work for it so it can work for you. I'll see you at the Top.

Disclaimer alert. I'm here to be your coach not your cheerleader. I'm your tour guide not your travel agent. What's the difference? Great question. A cheerleader stands on the sidelines and waves pompoms to motivate you. A coach is there to push you and do what's necessary to invoke you to live at your higher self. So, I'm not a pom-pom waver, I'm a purpose pusher.

What separates a travel agent from a tour guide is a travel agent will sell you a trip to somewhere they've never been. Whereas a tour guide will go with you along the journey because they are familiar with the places and geographical location necessary to get the maximum experience from the preferred destination, because they've been there. In other words, the tour guide has traversed the terrain and is familiar with the territory of where you want to go. Most travel agents work by commission and there's nothing wrong with being a travel agent, however, just check to see if they have been to the place or just basing their suggestions off the picture on the brochure.

Now what is Getting Ish Done:5 secrets to stop Procrastinating and get more Done in less time all about and what qualifies me to be a qualified expert at it????

Great Question?
Ish is just an acronym as I mentioned earlier, and a watchword pulled from today's colloquialisms that represents whatever you desire to be doing or get done. It's less about your ambitions and more focused around your assignment. Your Ish may be: Tangible or intangible.
Abstract or concrete, Physical, mental, or spiritual.
Finishing your degree or obtaining that certification.
It could be to lose weight or just tying up loose ends from other pending projects.
It's your ISH. You define it!
It may be small and minute' or humongous and ginormous, but whatever it is you get to decide it because it's your ISH! Period
I- is for intentional.
S- stands for strategic.
H- is for Habits that lead you to a course of action to accomplish the H3 ideology. H3 is the premise my mentor Dr. Dharius Daniel's teaches in his transformational programs of coaching leading and

speaking which means Getting it out of your head and your heart and into your hands. Again, allow me to be ridiculously clear. Ish is not just an acronym Ish about your assignment.

The Richest Place in the world is not a bank, it is the cemetery!

Allow me to share with you what happens to the average individual when attempting to accomplish their Ish. The best way I feel I can explain this is by using a snippet of something that happened to me many years ago. One of my best friends in the whole world was a gentleman by the name of C.L. Harvey. He was a brilliant communicator who had a mind that would not quit, and he could've been anything he wanted to be. We would talk every day just about if not every day we talked every other day. We even talked in the midnight hours because he was one of those people who challenged my mind and gave me fresh perspective, so talking to him was a great joy. One day I called him as was our norm, and for some reason my phone would not allow me to dial his number. After several failed attempts realizing my phone refused to allow me to dial his number, I went to the sprint store, which is now T-Mobile for a tech to look at my phone. I explained to the technician that I've tried repeatedly to reach my friends number, but for some reason my phone just would not dial it. It is as if it would allow me to call every number in my contacts list but his and a select few others. He took my phone back, examined it and returned within a few minutes. He said I believe I figured out your problem, for some reason, something you may have hit accidentally on your phone caused your phone to go to its default setting. The default settings are almost like when the phone comes from the factory in case of incident where people may get their wires crossed or do something that the phones computer or brain does not comprehend to protect itself, the phone reverts to its default setting. And then you must reset the phone, reload certain software and applications and your phone should work just fine. I learned a valuable lesson not only about phones that day, but I learned about us humans. Sometimes there are cases where we humans get our wires crossed up and to protect ourselves, we go to our default setting. I really preferred to call it default *settling*.

We as humans love familiarity and comfortability. Even when it is not beneficial. When it comes to procrastination for many it is like the default setting on the phone I once owned. Now you may ask. Charles, what is the secret? to stop procrastination.

The secret is there is no secret.

You can't wish for it; you have got to work for it. And if you are ready to do the soul work then you have the right book at the right time.

No Excuses. The Late Dr. Clay Evans once said, "we complain about being hungry with a loaf of Bread under our arm". I am convinced that we are living in an era where all of us should literally be **_EXCUSE FREE_**. As we now approach these 5 secrets or shall I say practices please remember to use your creative ingenuity to make them your own.

It's Not in The Land It's in The Man.

Too many times we overvalue others and undervalue ourselves. The above quote is something my pastor doctor frank Edward ray senior used to say all the time it's not in the land it's in the man. Meaning it's not about where you are it's always about who you are. One thing I love about being authentic is that I've learned to come to conversations motive free. It took me years to find out who I am, although I always knew who's I was. I now value myself and never underestimate what

God placed inside of me. As this generation can say stop sleeping on yourself, one of the shirts that is inside of our merch store says those who counted you out can't count. Then there's another shirt that we sell in our merch store that I love so much it says if they are sleeping on you tuck them in. And although that sounds very self-assuring, it should never be confused with arrogance. For confidence is normally looked at as arrogance by people who don't have any confidence. It's all about having God-fi-dence, it's a term I coined about godly confidence, which is believing in oneself like God believes in us. Once you truly awaken to who you are and all of the gift's talents and the anointing that God has placed in you then you can be fully alive and walking in any room and own the room for now you have permission to be comfortable in your own skin. I can't help but hear the words of my dear mother Shirley bond saying son don't ever let nobody low grade you. That was just her way of saying don't ever play seconds or second fiddle to anyone. I say this because you got Ish to do. And you will never get it done if you don't believe in you first. When I was a kid, they used to teach us these little stories and I will never forget the one about the little engine. Those of you who were born in my generation remember the little engine that could. It was the story about the little train engine who had to go up a mountain, and while going around the mountain she chugged along, and finally ran out of steam. Other engines came by but refused to help the little red engine. And finally, a little blue engine that was smaller came and was petitioned to help the little red engine get over the mountain. The moral of the story is the little blue engine was able to make it over the mountain and pull the other engine by saying the words I think I can I think I can I think I can. This little story written in the 1930's by Watty Piper was used to teach children the value of optimism and hard work. The bible declares in Proverbs 23:7 As a man thinks in his heart so is he. My friend, to get your Ish done not only do you need to get your head right let's get your heart right. And move from I think I can to I know I can. Its not in the land its in the man.

I shall never forget hearing the story of the Former 1st lady of Chicago Mayor Harold Washington. He made history in April of 1983 when he was selected as the first African American mayor of the city of Chicago. Those who can remember these years were a time where we had full service filling stations. For those of you born post 80's era these were not just self serve gast stations like we have today but there was a time when you pulled up to a filling station for fuel you didn't have to get out of your car if you pulled on the full service side or lane. An attendant would come out pump your gas, check your tires, cap off your fluids and clean your windshield. Well the stories told that when Mayor Washington and his wife were getting their car fueled his wife looked startled as the gentlemen cleaned their windshield. It was as if she had seen a ghost. Noticing a shift in her demeanor he asked her what was wrong. And she shrugged it off and said, "oh nothing." Not wanting to let it go he prodded her until she finally said "if you must know the gentlemen who pumped our gas was the first love of my life. Mayor Washington in a humorous way said, "well I bet your glad you didn't marry him." She responded, "why do you say that?" He said, "because if you had married him, you wouldn't be married to the first black mayor of Chicago you would be married to a service station attendant" and her response was stellar, she proceeded to say, "no I wouldn't, because if I had married him, he would've been the 1st black mayor of Chicago." The point is, she understood what she brought to the table. As you go forth to get your Ish done, know your worth and then add tax! You owe YOU!

Lastly, before I delve into these 5 ways to stop procrastinating and get more done in less time. I feel the need to reiterate that success is a relevant term. I can't stress this enough because success is different for everyone. Only you can determine and define what your ISH is and what success looks like through your lens. If you don't you will live your life allowing others to dictate your pallets. I learned a very valuable lesson about our Americanized idea about success from my friend and brother Dr. Jamal Harrison Bryant, I'll call it success from another perspective. Dr. Jamal Bryant pastor of the mega church New Birth in Atlanta came to preach for me in 2021 and while at the restaurant that evening with some very close friends Pastors Rickey and Sheila Floyd and Bishop Edgar Vann. He tells the story of his 1st major crusade in Africa. He was taken aback by the introduction of the Pastor who was on the ticket to introduce him. He said he sat there for 30 minutes or more as they spoke of the guy who introduced him and brought this gentlemen up to the podium and had his children come up and literally read off several of his children's accomplishments and the person went on and on giving accolades to this pastor and his family until Jamal said he leaned over and inquired to the person next to him and said is this normal for them to take this long introducing the introducer of the key note. And the person responded Dr. Bryant in our country your success is not measured by the size of your congregation or the square footage of your facilities. But in our custom, you are successful according to how well you steward your family and if you have successfully raised your family then you are revered in our nation as successful and are to be celebrated. The point is success in that country is far different from ours. We gage success by what's in the driveway or in our garages and by what kind of clothes and brands we can boast. When the truth is to some people success looks like a fleet of expensive cars to someone else success is just having reliable transportation. To some people success is owning a 15-room mansion, to someone else success is getting their own apartment in their own name. my point is never let anyone else define what success looks like to you. and when you arrive at whatever success you may achieve. Please remain humble and as I said earlier never let getting ahead go to your head. Just remember nobody likes braggarts!

Well, here it is. In my opinion, these are the top five ways to stop procrastinating and get more done in less time. Please note, these are not the only five, I just believe these are the top five.

GETTING ISH DONE

5 SECRETS TO STOP PROCRASTINATING & GET MORE DONE IN LESS TIME!

CHARLES BOND
Forward by Dr. Kerwin B. Lee

Getting ISH Done

Step One: Decide What ISH You Want More!

"An Inch of Movement is worth more than a mile of Intent."

A little boy in the rural lived next door to a marksman (a person skilled at shooting, especially with a pistol or rifle). The little boy went over to his neighbor's home one day and asked him would he teach him how to be a great marksman. The little boy mentioned that he noticed all the trees in the wooded area behind their two houses that the marksman would use for target practice had bullseye targets on each tree and each target was hit right in the center of each bullseye. He asked the neighbor how he'd manage to hit each target directly in the center of the bullseye on every single tree. The neighbor responded "oh that's simple, I shot the tree first and then went and painted a bullseye around the bullet hole. The moral of this story is this is the manner of how some people live their lives. They shoot at some stuff and then paint around it as if that was their target in the first place.

I am telling you that if you are going to accomplish your ISH you cannot go through life aimlessly shooting at stuff and what ever you hit, you claim that's what you were aiming at from the beginning. Getting ISH done requires you to DECIDE what ISH you want more. Notice I said decide and not choose. Because when you choose that means to pick one. Nope, deciding is deeper than choosing. Decide is a compound word. DE- meaning off and CIDE- means to cut, literally you must cut yourself off from any other option than going through with your ISH, and seeing your Ish get done.

Now that we have a premise in this first step allow me to explain why this is the most important step. We live in a society where multi-tasking has become a way of life. Now don't get me wrong, I in no way am judging demonizing or attacking people who are able to as my father used to say, "can chew bubble gum and walk at the same time." What I am saying is most people attempt to do so much and never master focusing on one thing well at a time. Our society has programmed us to become addicted to DOING. The reason I say you need to decide what ISH matters most is because if your focus is divided, nine times out of ten you will not expedite nor execute your tasks or your ISH well. It's possible, however, still not in many cases advantageous. Please keep in mind there is always the exception where you have many people that operate best under pressure or in organized chaos, but still the effectiveness of their Ish and their ability to get things done in excellence may be questionable. So, when you decide what Ish matters most or shall I say prioritize your Ish, then you will become a rock star and procrastination will no longer rule or ruin your productivity level. I would rather do a thing right than be forced to do it over.

As I afore mentioned we have become addicted to doing. I remember going to a conference years ago in Washington D.C. and the facilitator taught a principle that I teach now to my coaching clients. The principle is what I describe in my book "I'm @ Peace: 7 ways to eliminate excuses and remove the roadblocks that hinder your happiness" and the principle is called stop GETTING, HAVING, DOING. Yes, that's the cycle we get caught up in because of todays cultural imagery of wanting more. We get caught up in the cycles of getting, having, doing, getting, having, doing, getting having doing , until it becomes a way of life. Yet the underlying truth is it keeps us in the mindset of constantly grinding and allowing culture to paint for us what success looks like. The problem with this kind of constant aggression is, there's nothing wrong with wanting more or better, the problem is what is your why. I mean are you in competition with someone, are you attempting to prove someone wrong or are you just a natural born over achiever. All I personally advise is just know your reasoning and your why. Because I have known people who have spent so much time attempting to make a living that they forget to live. The tragedy of the getting, having, doing mindset is that we get so addicted to doing that if there's nothing to do we say we are bored so we create something to do because we are addicted to doing. Here's the challenge. ALL ACTIVITY IS NOT PRODUCTIVITY. Also, there is no true peace and fulfillment in getting, having, doing because we were not created to be a human getting, a human having, nor a human doing, we were created to be human beings. The biggest question you must ask is when was the last time that you were truly content just being. Being present, being still, being mindful of the moment you are in. Most people like me must make our brains turn off. Stop getting, having, doing and learn how to BE. And you'll not only have more peace but you will also have clarity of scope so you can get more of your Ish done because you decided what Ish mattered most.

Now I hope those main two previous points stick with you and become a part of your mantra. All activity is not productivity and learning the power of being.

Define why your Ish matters?

Knowing your why is important because most people spend their lives mimicking others. And as I've learned Imitation is limitation. When you are living out loud you are truly in a place of real authenticity when you are ridiculously clear on your why. This book is to drive home the fact that your assignment is too important, and some things will never happen to you until you first learn how to happen to them. When you decide what your Ish is, and you are clear on your why you can operate with a certain kind of assurance and authority that make getting your Ish done more realistic.

I want to add a simple addendum to this section of deciding what Ish you want more. As a believer in God and His word I believe it's also equally important to know your enemies why. Yes, every great fighter studies the style and gait of his adversary or opponent. Our enemy has a why and knowing his why also impacts us getting our Ish done. My reason for saying this is we must never underestimate Satan and all his imps. But on the flip side we must not over think the enemy or his seeming power. Satan normally fights us in three main areas. He fights or attacks us as individuals because we are his replacement, and no one likes the replacement. He was kicked out of heaven and God said I will make me a man who will worship me in spirit and in truth. So he hates us because we are his replacement. Secondly, he attacks us in the area of relationships. Rather its romantic between husbands and wives, or significant others, or it could be relationships with siblings or friendships and relationship. His why is because he was never allowed to enjoy true authentic relationship so he resents and hates us because we do. Lastly he attacks us in the area of worship. That's why its always an issues between church members and ministries because he got kicked out of the only church he was a member of. So knowing the enemies why is just as important as knowing who the enemy is.

Stop looking over the fence!

He who chases many rabbits catches none is one of the most factual truths I personally had to face on my journey to ending my battle with procrastination. The truth of the matter is not knowing what Ish mattered most and not being self-aware that I was too impetuous to focus caused me some very expensive lessons along my journey. If you haven't gotten it by now this is not a book about one and done projects or momentary satisfaction. The main inference is about you living fully and present because although I'm not a gambling man I am still willing to bet that many of the people who struggle with seeing things through suffer from ADHD or maybe some form of attention deficit. The truth, however, is although society wants to over medicate us, we must do the hard soul work of getting still long enough to be honest with ourselves to ask the hard questions like why am I like this or what led to my frame of thinking this way?

One of the most important steps you will take in deciding what Ish matters most is when you stop looking over the fence. If you haven't figured it out by now, I am a true southerner in every since of the word. My mother was born in Mississippi, and my dad in rural Tennessee. All I knew up until a certain point was southern lingo. One of the things you pick up in the deep south is the older generations had a unique way of making statements with out using a lot of words. Statements like the pot cant call the kettle black, meaning no one has any room to talk about others in a condescending way. Or, and six in one hand or a half dozen in the other meaning something that kind of pans out to be the same thing no matter how you spin it. Likewise, when I say stop looking over the fence, I'm basically attempting to get you delivered from this disease called comparison-itis. It's a disease that you will not find on the CDC (center for disease control) website, however it is just as deadly as any terminal illness you find. I venture to say it's worse because of medical advances, most diseases are treatable but this one is most assuredly terminal. One of the main causes of procrastination is we spend so much time distracted by comparing our lives to the images that we are inundated with constantly within our culture. And I will discuss this further in the next step of how we fall for the okie doke of the illusion trap of Hollywood and the powers that be. Yet indulge me for a moment because you are not the only one who constantly or occasionally glances over the fence and from your initial assessment you assume the grass is greener. First put this in your notes, most people rather it be on television, social media etc. never post their failures. Mostly all people post their successes or their illusion of success by showing their front. I learned years ago from Universal Studios that they have these movie sets and at first glance it appears to be a whole town or street scene with a lot of buildings. But if you walk through the actual front door of what appears to be a salon, or hotel etc. it is only a front. Because on the inside it's just shallow, empty, or propped up. It's called a front. It's meant to appear to be something it's not. And with all due respect, if imitation reflects life, the truth is most people who are not authentic or haven't matured to the point of understanding life does not have to be a competition. Then you are most likely to see people who only show you, their front. The ole school rappers used to say in street terms "stop frontin."

1 Samuel 8:1-5 (KJV)

[1] And it came to pass, when Samuel was old, that he made his sons judges over Israel.

[2] Now the name of his firstborn was Joel; and the name of his second, Abiah: they were judges in Beersheba.

[3] And his sons walked not in his ways, but turned aside after lucre, and took bribes, and perverted judgment.

[4] Then all the elders of Israel gathered themselves together, and came to Samuel unto Ramah,

[5] And said unto him, Behold, thou art old, and thy sons walk not in thy ways: now make us a king to judge us like all the nations.

This particular passage found in 1st Samuel chapter 8 is a prime example of what comparison-itis looks like. The children of Israel Gods chosen people had a righteous conflict of interest issue with the sons of Samuel the prophet, who had set up his sons to become Judges over Gods people. The problem became that Samuels sons were not like him. For they took bribes and allowed the right to be wrong and wrong to be right. Basically, they tainted the system God originally designed because of their own greed and immaturity. And although the children of Israel had a right to protest, their motive was the issue. They were looking over the fence at the other tribes and said specifically to the prophet when they met with him to explain their issue with his sons. They said make us a king **(LIKE ALL THE OTHER NATIONS)**. How many times have we did the same thing? Based our decisions, choices, or desires on what someone else had. And later they would regret this decision because of how the story plays out, yet the point remains that they're why was not healthy. If you don't stop looking over the fence you will sometimes self-sabotage or ruin your dreams, goals etc. because you spend too much time looking over the fence. Looking over the fence will have you focusing so much on what you lost until you won't pay attention to what you have left. Looking over the fence will have you believing a lie that the grass is greener on the other side of the fence, when the truth is your grass can be just as green if you water it and keep it cut. Looking over the fence will have you thinking that everyone else's marriage is a dream and yours is a nightmare on Elm Street. Looking over the fence will have you thinking that your present situation is a curse, and everyone is happy except you. Looking over the fence will have you wearing clothes not meant for your body type or shape. It will have you wearing hairstyles that don't look good on you, or even purchasing cars you can't afford or trying to live in a zip code that leaves you house poor once you pay your rent or mortgage. Adam and Eve got evicted from the garden of Eden looking over the fence.

David lost his joy and brought a curse on his house by looking over the fence at a woman sun-bathing. The prodigal son left home too soon thinking the far country had better accommodations than his father's house so he left home pre-maturely all because he was looking over the fence. Husbands have lost good wives and wives have lost great husbands looking over the fence. People have left great jobs and left great careers looking over the fence. Only to discover that what they had was not that bad after all they had just invested in it. Countless people (self-included) fell for the trick of the enemy and thought they needed a new, situation, a new spouse, a new job, a new body, a new gadget, a new start in another city, when the truth is you need a new you and a new perspective and to inner vest in your dream. Because you have Ish to DO! It's like one time there was this pasture on a farm and in the pasture was a bull who had several fertile cows in his pasture. As a matter of fact, all he had to do was eat grass and service those fertile cows in his pasture. However, there was a bob wire fence that separated his pasture from the farm next doors pasture and this bull would keep his nose over by the fence lusting, looking, and lurking because in the pasture next door way over in a distance it appeared to be two fertile cows. One day after not being able to take it any longer curiosity got the best of the bull. He made up his mind that he wanted to have those two fertile cows' way over in the other pasture. So, he got him a running start and one day he went and jumped that bob wire fence. He ended up injuring himself, and he was bleeding profusely but it didn't matter because he had made it over the fence. And he ran over toward those two cows and the closer he got, he realized that they were bulls too. The moral is you may be better where you are than where you think you want to be. Stop looking over the fence and focus on what is at hand, so that you can get your Ish done and stop daydreaming over an illusion.

The Final Frontier

The most effective question to help you start to sort through life's noise so that you can accomplish the things God has assigned you to do is to ask the one question that is above all questions concerning your Ish. Is this the Ish for me? Basically, are you doing what it is you desire and discern is the assignment for you. or are you living vicariously through someone else or for someone else. Because you would be surprised at the people who are living a lie, which is just as bad as telling one. Decide from this day forward that you will live authentically and fully present to the life God desires for you to have. Remember he said he came that you might have life and that more abundantly. So how do I decide what Ish matters most? In a nutshell here is the answer. Prayer. Pause and pray by petitioning God and simply asking is this what I'm supposed to be doing? I've learned over time not to even ask God to bless what I am doing, but rather ask God to allow me to do what He is blessing. Someone asked once. What is God doing? The answer was working. What was he working on they asked? The answer was His will. Where is He working it at, they asked? Inside of us was the response.

Someone lied, we do not have ten fingers. We have eight phalanges and two pollexes' which are incorporated through prehensile cognition. Basically, this normally means anything you pick up without your thumbs you drop it. Anything you pick up with your thumbs makes it easier to hold on to. Likewise, anything you pick up without God, you drop it and anything you pick up with God you hold on to it. The hymnologist said it best in that old hymn of the church:

What a friend we have in Jesus,
All our sins and griefs to bear!
What a privilege to carry
Everything *to God in prayer!*
Oh, what peace we often forfeit,
Oh, what needless pain we bear,
All because we do not carry
Everything *to God in prayer!*
Have we trials and temptations?
Is there trouble anywhere?
We should never be discouraged—
Take it to the Lord in prayer.
Can we find a friend so faithful,
Who will all our sorrows share?
Jesus knows our every weakness.
Take it to the Lord in prayer.

Step Two: What Ish Are You Allowing in Your Head?

When purpose is not known abuse is inevitable
~Dr. Miles Monroe

This secret or step shall I say is crucial to getting your Ish done. Get your head back in the game. There are 360 references in the bible to the head and 96 times the bible refers or mentions the word mind. I believe that once you think about the stuff you really think about you will be one step closer to getting your Ish done. The adage says that leaders are readers, however that's only partially true. Leaders are learners. Because if you only read that's the ability to consume information. Yet if you only consume information and never comprehend information, and then apply the knowledge you've learned you will be a walking storage unit. Now let's take a moment to overstand and not understand the things we allow in our headspace and why.

Wow I know you were probably shocked when I used the word overstand. Truth is the word overstand faded into disuse centuries ago although it was replaced by the word understand. I often study etymology and discovered the word "understand" comes from Old English "understandan," which means "to comprehend, grasp the idea of." The "under" part implies "among, between," while the "standan" part means "to stand, or to be situated." So, "understand" originally meant "to stand among or between." The term "overstand" is not commonly used in modern English, but it has been used in some dialects and contexts to mean "to understand

11

thoroughly, to have full comprehension of." The "over" part implies "beyond, surpassing," so "overstand" would mean "to stand beyond or surpass in understanding." This usage is not as widespread as "understand," and it's more of a niche or archaic term.

Now let's overstand the stuff that goes in our heads. I often teach and echo the scriptures. Which teaches us to guard our minds. The mind can be the enemy's workshop if allowed, therefore the mind is a battleground and not a playground. What you allow in your head will determine the direction of your actions. Because the Ish (intentional, strategies, and habits) you allow in your head is more than a notion it is mental training of your subconscious and in most cases, people are unaware that it's even happening. The focus is knowing the purpose of everything you do and why you do it.

I go back to the opening quote by Dr. Miles Monroe, who taught us that when purpose is not known abuse is inevitable. The point becomes, most people operate unaware of why they do the things they do. So, the problem that lies here is twofold. First the average person is living their life with no real game plan, sense of direction, or knowledge of purpose. Secondly the average person is unaware that they serve an agenda of the wealthy and power brokers of today's mainstream culture that is anti-strategic intentional individualism. Meaning we live in a culture and society of mimickers.

The question becomes who am I? Why am I here? And what am I here for? If you don't know the answer to any of these, you will only get the Ish of others done and not your own Ish. Because everyone should know their purpose. Or someone will use you for a purpose you were not created for, and most likely you will be serving their purpose and not your own. Allow me to use laymen's terms. Have you ever used a butter knife for a screwdriver? Or the heel of a shoe for a hammer? Or a mason jar for a drinking glass? The point is these items can be used to improvise in all the scenarios mentioned, but they still are being misused outside of what the creator or inventor had in mind. Can they still be effective? Yes. However, not as effective as they are in the purpose for which they were created. Yes, you can use the heel of a shoe to tack something down or in a wall, but the shoe was not designed with being a makeshift hammer in mind. It was designed to be worn on your foot. Yes, you can attempt to screw something in using a butter knife however a screwdriver would be more effective because it was designed to screw things in. I'm sure you get the point which is when people are used outside of purpose they are abused, used, mishandled, mismanaged and unconsidered.

Genesis 1:26-28 (KJV)
26 And God said, Let us make man in our image, after our likeness: and let them have dominion over the fish of the sea, and over the fowl of the air, and over the cattle, and over all the earth, and over every creeping thing that creepeth upon the earth.
27 So God created man in his own image, in the image of God created he him; male and female created he them.
28 And God blessed them, and God said unto them, Be fruitful, and multiply, and replenish the earth, and subdue it: and have dominion over the fish of the sea, and over the fowl of the air, and over every living thing that moveth upon the earth.

Notice how we were made. In Gods image and likeness. Those who have any theological acumen understand that image means to look like, and likeness means to be like. So, god basically wanted us to be little versions of him here on earth. Thus Jesus said:

> ***John 10:34-38 (KJV)***
> *³⁴ Jesus answered them, Is it not written in your law, I said, Ye are gods?*
> *³⁵ If he called them gods, unto whom the word of God came, and the scripture cannot be broken;*
> *³⁶ Say ye of him, whom the Father hath sanctified, and sent into the world, Thou blasphemest; because I said, I am the Son of God?*
> *³⁷ If I do not the works of my Father, believe me not.*
> *³⁸ But if I do, though ye believe not me, believe the works: that ye may know, and believe, that the Father is in me, and I in him.*

Jesus was quoting Psalm 82:6 and its literally means we are little versions of God. Like we are little versions of our parents. We are also little gods. Someone once said that's why they call us a masterpiece because we are pieces of the Master (God). God was a creator; we are creatives who create out of what was already created by the creator.

But please do not forget he made us and then gave us our purpose in Genesis chapter one verses 26-28 he created us to not only be like and look like him, but He also gave us dominion which is defined as having power or is synonymous with rule. However, let's be clear dominion is not ownership or the idea of complete control as much as it signifies stewardship, authority, and care taking. And even in this he gave them dominion over everything on the earth except one another. Yet please be very clear. That's not to suggest that God doesn't have natural order however the idea was never to control others. And that's some people's issue in relationships; they want to control the other person and the problem is it takes all our time trying to control ourselves less known another human being. He gave us dominion over beasts not beings, over land not loved ones, over places not people.

> [28] *And God blessed them, and God said unto them, Be fruitful, and multiply, and replenish the earth, and subdue it: and have dominion over the fish of the sea, and over the fowl of the air, and over every living thing that moveth upon the earth.*

Now here comes the details of the dominion.

Be fruitful. Let's look at it slower. Fruit-full. Where do you find fruit at the grocery store or supermarket? Its normally in the produce section. So being fruitful is about being productive. Which points to the second purpose of humans which is growing things, why do you think he placed Adam and Eve in a garden called Eden? Multiply means to increase greatly in number. Replenish if you look at it, it's a compound word re is the root word for again and plenish is from the Latin word "plenir" which is the English word fill. So, replenish means to refill it again. Subdue is the word hupotasso meaning to place in order or to place under in an orderly fashion. It's the picture of someone neatly rearranging scattered objects or organizing something. And then he reiterates what he placed the humans over fish, fowl, and four footed and two footed beasts. Not over each other. Because when man understands his purpose as husband and woman understands her purpose as wife, there is never any confusion about power, authority, or order because the bible gives each person their purpose and instructions.

I hope that so far you have a pretty good grasp on your purpose. You were designed, created, and commissioned to take all of the internal gifts, knowledge, talents, skills, and external accoutrements and GET ISH DONE!

Now let's look at what Ish you allow in your head. I mentioned earlier that to get Ish done not only does one need to guard your mind gate, meaning watch what you allow and who you allow to get inside your head. I also mentioned you must begin to think about what you think about. Allow me to explain. The word muse means to think. When you place an a in front of the word muse it spells amuse which means not to think. So, it's tantamount to what happens when you go to an amusement park, and it seems like you are having so much fun time flies by. That's because you were being amused so there are no clocks in an amusement park because the focus is to get you to not think about time and have fun and of course spend more money. The point is simple when you amuse people it distracts them from thinking. The challenge is if you are going to get your Ish done, you must be a thinker for yourself and not allow others to do your thinking for you. which in turn requires knowing and being self-aware of what Ish you allow into your head.

Aretha Franklin tried to tell us!

Although the song think is about self-awareness and free thinking, the overall thought behind the hook of the song is what we should take away which is about thinking about what is being done to us by others. I owe it to my pastor Dr. Frank E. Ray Sr. for teaching me years ago that words tell you what they want you to know that's why I emphasize the Ish we allow in our heads.

Think about this. Have you ever considered that we are being directed daily by the powers that be. Now before you dismiss this as conspiracy theory hear me out. The average person is sometimes clueless as to why they do some of the things they do. Let's take fashion for instance or choices. Have you ever thought about why we wear certain styles or fads? For instance, why do most men walk around with beards today? Its because of the power of T.V.

Hollywood has an agenda. There are billions if not trillions of dollars in fashion and brands being made all the time. The execs in Hollywood know that the average person doesn't have a vision of their own, so they give you a vision with a device called a television pronounce (Tell-ah-vison). So they tell us what to wear or what's in style by parading their wears on our favorite, actors, music artists, athletes, and influencers. Because if you see something over and over repeatedly it's called subconscious impartation. Meaning the law of what goes in must come out and couple that with the fact that we mostly mimic what we see modeled in front of us, so this is done through television programming. Yes, we are all being programmed. Let's take something as simple as radio. It is called radio programming. Have you noticed you can hear a song over and over and without ever having looked at the physical lyrics you go around singing or humming the tunes you like because you can't get it out of your head. They know that repetition is the mother of all learning.

That's right, there's an agenda therefore we must think about the Ish we allow to get into our heads. Readers are leaders, and leaders are learners. As we prepare to get our Ish done, take note of the habits you have and begin to ask questions of yourself like why I am this way or why do I think a certain way? Are you a free thinker? Or do you just follow suit? Success leaves clues so if you are going to follow a trend follow successful people. As I forementioned, its nothing wrong with being a copycat if you copy the right cat. Just know why. And think about it.

Getting ISH Done

Step Three: Write Ish Down!

"The shortest pencil is better than the longest memory."

Habakkuk 2:2-3 (KJV)
² And the LORD answered me, and said, **<u>Write</u>** the vision, and make it plain upon tables, that he may run that readeth it. ³ For the vision is yet for an appointed time, but at the end it shall speak, and not lie: though it tarry, wait for it; because it will surely come, it will not tarry.

Habakkuk 2:2-3 (TLB)
² And the Lord said to me, "**<u>Write</u>** my answer (vision) on a billboard, large and clear, so that anyone can read it at a glance and rush to tell the others. ³ But these things I plan won't happen right away. Slowly, steadily, surely, the time approaches when the vision will be fulfilled. If it seems slow, do not despair, for these things will surely come to pass. Just be patient! They will not be overdue a single day!

Habakkuk 2:2-3 (AMP)
² And the Lord answered me and said, **<u>Write</u>** the vision and engrave it so plainly upon tablets that everyone who passes may [be able to] read [it easily and quickly] as he hastens by. ³ For the vision is yet for an appointed time and it hastens to the end [fulfillment]; it will not deceive or disappoint. Though it tarry, wait [earnestly] for it, because it will surely come; it will not be behindhand on its appointed day.

I placed this passage in a couple of different versions because I wanted you to have a more modern read of this ancient text, however the one thing each version I looked it up in had in common was the phrase write the vision. One of my greatest influences of all times is Bishop Timothy Clark who taught me the principle of writing has no substitute for you remember what you write.

We often tend to forget to remember. This is because the average person has approximately 60,000 thoughts a day. That's a lot to have on one's mind. This is probably the shortest of all the five secrets to getting Ish done because it is cut and dry. Write Ish down. I want to give you the 3 A's of writing Ish down that I believe will not only be a game changer but also a great asset to your repertoire of knowledge.

I live by a "Things to do" list not as a slave to the list but because it helps me in several ways to stay true to my commitments. And if I can be honest the older, I get the more I realize that age plays a vital role in acuity and sharpness, so I need to always stack the deck in my corner.

1. **I write Ish down because it helps my ACCOUNTABILITY!**

You must realize that not only does the average person get bombarded with several thoughts on a constant basis, but we also must factor in distractions. A lot of people have now been diagnosed with things like ADD attention deficit disorder. And although this is a clinical disorder the truth is even extremely focused people are not exempt from the occasional distraction here and there. I personally went to a printer and had them to make me this tear off note pads that read:

Charles' Things that must be done!

1. <u>Pray / Meditate / Positive Confessions / Work Out</u>

2. _____

3. _____

And as you can see from my example, my first 4 things are what I do every morning not just out of routine but because I practice the principles that I teach. The reason my first four things are consistent every day is because the H in Ish stands for Habit, healthy ones might I add. This came about because I used to struggle with morbid obesity, and I hated working out. Going to the gym was to me like kryptonite was to superman. One day I read this book by Brian Tracy Entitled Eat That Frog. And in his book, he touted that if the hardest thing you had to do every day was eat a frog, eat the biggest ugliest, slimiest one first and everything you had to do after that should be relatively easy. Well, you must determine what your frog is. For me my frog was working out or going to the gym. So, I procrastinated. One day after a doctor's visit I had ballooned up to a whooping 553lbs. yes you read that correctly I weighed a quarter of a ton. I decided that day to eat my frog. I went to the gym and started working out at a pace that was for me. And before you knew it, I was addicted to going to the gym and what started out as only being able to do a quarter mile on the treadmill I worked my way up to 3 miles a day. My point is writing it down helped me be accountable to myself.

2. **Secondly Writing my Ish down helped me track my ACTIVITY.**

If you remember earlier, I mentioned all activity is not necessarily productivity. Again, I want to reiterate that everyone is different, so you may not deal with staying focused or seeing your Ish through. Yet tracking activity or even committing is a problem for a lot of people. Well don't feel alone. When you write your Ish down you can if you are very organized or contemplative, you are able to write things down potentially to prioritize what tasks need attention immediately and which ones are not as urgent. There are several Life I hack tools that I teach in the framework of my coaching that assist you with getting ahead quicker. Remember if it does not have anything to do with your Ish it does not deserve to make the list. Also, when I write my Ish down it also makes a mental inscription or mental note that this is something that deserves my efforts and my energy. Here is a tweetable moment. Don't get involved with things that don't help you evolve.

3. **I write my Ish down because it lastly gives me a sense of ACCOMPLISHMENT.**

My friend, I can't begin to explain the sense of accomplishment I feel when I complete one of the things on my to do list or shall I say I finish some of my Ish. And the sheer joy of drawing a line through it is such a blessing. That's right when you complete a task or see your Ish through then it's time to celebrate the victory. No matter how big or small the task, the mere fact that you didn't procrastinate, delay, or put it off is a blessing within itself.

I quote again the secret to your success is hidden in your daily routine. Well let's change it up and say the secret to your success is revealed in our written routine! I know this principle works. I wrote down on my things to do list months a few months ago on an airplane that I wanted to write a book and do an e-course about Getting Ish done. That was in October of 2023. I wrote it in the inkpad note taking app on my cellphone and now here it is in 2024 coming to pass.

Write it, walk in it, win it, witness it.

The final reason I am such a proponent of writing your Ish down is not so that you will become a slave to the list. Allow me to be honest I fell into this trap in my earlier days of making to do list. However, I learned that life can through you some unexpected curve balls, so we must allow some wiggle room in life to make necessary adjustments in the ebb and flow of things. My reasoning for writing it down and yes, I am clear we are in a technological age that's moving toward a paperless society, for we dare not kill more trees. So if you must use your apps, mobile devices and things like "todoist"an app that touts itself as the world's number one task manager for those seeking to organize life and work. but let's not forget our why. My list has not just become my check off itemized documentation so that I can feel accomplished and have bragging rights of pride and arrogance. Remember no one likes braggarts and showoffs. I told you earlier there's a big difference between having pride and being full of it. But our list should also serve as a reminder of the integrity we owe to ourselves. There are several days where I don't complete tasks on my things to do list and in those cases the items just move to the next day. I want to conclude this step by reminding you what the text says:

Habakkuk 2:2-3 (KJV)
² And the LORD answered me, and said, Write the vision, and make it plain upon tables, that he may run that

readeth it. ³ *For the vision is yet for an appointed time, but at the end it shall speak, and not lie: though it tarry, wait for it; because it will surely come, it will not tarry.*

The principle is clear Write the vision. Better yet write your vision and not the one preloaded by Hollywood. Write it means to put it on **_PAPER_** as one of my favorite songs by Reverend Al Green and Ms. Ann Nesbit. That's officializing it if I may use that term. Secondly make it **_PLAIN_**. Then thirdly the text says **_PUBLISH_** it now here is the key to this step and the secret sauce. Rather you use an app or just a good ole pencil or pen and write it down, which carves it into your subconscious. Making it plain is adding some details, benchmarks, and boundaries as well as steps that will help you accomplish your Ish. For example, let's say your goal is to create a vision board then here is how my list (again everyone is different you do it your way because it's your Ish).

Things to do list for today.
1. **Go to the art supply store and purchase vision board/poster board.**
2. **Purchase markers, glue sticks, magazines that capture things I like (like pictures of houses, cars, clothes, vacation destinations, and even intangible things like successful marriages etc. how you see success etc.**
3. **I will carve out one hour to begin to cut out pictures in magazines and prepare them to go on my vision board.**

The point is each thing you do gets you closer to your ISH.
Now when the bible says in the above-mentioned passage in Habakkuk about making it plain that means write in details. Here is a freebie. Don't be afraid to dream in color and write BIG stuff or

goals on your list. Be audacious and stop living your life like a scary cat. The bible says that God would supply our need. Not our greed but the word need is plural. And I love how he said he would do it, not according to your resources, or what's in your savings account, but God will do it according to his riches in Glory. That means I don't shrink my vision down to mediocrity, I blow it up to a God sized dream on a level that is according to my faith. So go big or go home. I used to preach a sermon out of a passage found in 2nd Kings chapter 3:1-18;

2 Kings 3:1-18 (KJV)
^{1} Now Jehoram the son of Ahab began to reign over Israel in Samaria the eighteenth year of Jehoshaphat king of Judah, and reigned twelve years.
^{2} And he wrought evil in the sight of the LORD; but not like his father, and like his mother: for he put away the image of Baal that his father had made.
^{3} Nevertheless he cleaved unto the sins of Jeroboam the son of Nebat, which made Israel to sin; he departed not therefrom.
^{4} And Mesha king of Moab was a sheepmaster, and rendered unto the king of Israel an hundred thousand lambs, and an hundred thousand rams, with the wool.
^{5} But it came to pass, when Ahab was dead, that the king of Moab rebelled against the king of Israel.
^{6} And king Jehoram went out of Samaria the same time, and numbered all Israel.
^{7} And he went and sent to Jehoshaphat the king of Judah, saying, The king of Moab hath rebelled against me: wilt thou go with me against Moab to battle? And he said, I will go up: I am as thou art, my people as thy people, and my horses as thy horses.

⁸ And he said, Which way shall we go up? And he answered, The way through the wilderness of Edom.

⁹ So the king of Israel went, and the king of Judah, and the king of Edom: and they fetched a compass of seven days' journey: and there was no water for the host, and for the cattle that followed them.

¹⁰ And the king of Israel said, Alas! that the LORD hath called these three kings together, to deliver them into the hand of Moab!

¹¹ But Jehoshaphat said, Is there not here a prophet of the LORD, that we may enquire of the LORD by him? And one of the king of Israel's servants answered and said, Here is Elisha the son of Shaphat, which poured water on the hands of Elijah.

¹² And Jehoshaphat said, The word of the LORD is with him. So the king of Israel and Jehoshaphat and the king of Edom went down to him.

¹³ And Elisha said unto the king of Israel, What have I to do with thee? get thee to the prophets of thy father, and to the prophets of thy mother. And the king of Israel said unto him, Nay: for the LORD hath called these three kings together, to deliver them into the hand of Moab.

¹⁴ And Elisha said, As the LORD of hosts liveth, before whom I stand, surely, were it not that I regard the presence of Jehoshaphat the king of Judah, I would not look toward thee, nor see thee.

¹⁵ But now bring me a minstrel. And it came to pass, when the minstrel played, that the hand of the LORD came upon him.

¹⁶ And he said, Thus saith the LORD, Make this valley full of ditches.

17 For thus saith the LORD, Ye shall not see wind, neither shall ye see rain; yet that valley shall be filled with water, that ye may drink, both ye, and your cattle, and your beasts.
18 And this is but a light thing in the sight of the LORD: he will deliver the Moabites also into your hand.

This passage is tantamount because it was about a king who took over when his dad died, and one of the smaller kingdoms stop paying taxes to this wicked king. So he writes a letter to a righteous king Jehosaphat and asks him to join him in teaching the rebellious king a lesson. Jehoshaphat the righteous king agrees to go with his army and help the wicked king, in the meantime they also engage a third king and his army, and they take this 7-day journey on their way to do battle and they ran out of water for three armies and their beasts and to make matters worst they are in the desert. One of the groups mentions there is a prophet who can tell them what to do and so the three kings go visit the prophet who basically tells the other kings if it wasn't for the fact that he regarded the righteous king he wouldn't be entertaining them, which says a lot about your character and the company we keep. However, the prophet prays on their behalf and the answer he gets back is tell them that if they want water **_make the valley full of ditches_**. And God would fill whatever they dug and give them the victory in battle.

My point for taking you the long way around is I want you to take note that they chose to here, heed, and honor the right directions and, their victory was tied to their ability to follow the instructions. They would receive big amounts of water only if they dug big ditches or trenches as one version says. I entitled the sermon "Can You Dig It?" Always remember God doesn't necessarily always give you what you pray for, He gives you what you are prepared for. My advice when writing your vision is to dig a ditch as the passage instructed make this valley full of ditches. In other words, don't go dig a spoon size puddle, go get a bulldozer and dig a lake size area, in preparation for overflow. For the question is not can God fill it, but rather can you dig it?

Now that hopefully your faith has been stretched, let's get back to this vision business. I hope you've prayed, prioritized, put it on paper, and made it plain. Which again is not only the details, but also being specific in what it is you are setting out to accomplish. Stop praying general prayers and be specific with God. Don't attempt to bring God down to your level but rather ascribe up to His level. God is about details. The sun is 93 million miles away from planet earth, scientists agree if it were one degree closer, we would all burn up, and if it was one degree further from our planet, we would all freeze. Now tell me that's not a God who pays attention to details. Therefore, be specific, but lastly writing the vision is not only about details but about discipline. Most people don't have a vision for a thing and so I wonder why you are so shocked that things turn out the way they do. If you are going to get your Ish done, you've got to learn how to be visionary.

Stephen Covey wrote a very popular book entitled the 7 habits of Highly successful people, and it was the 2nd habit that resonated with me most. It stated, to simply begin with the end in mind. In other words, mentally envision the desired outcome of a project and work from there. It's what movie producers sometimes do; they shoot the last scenes first and then go back and film in a way that the story progresses toward the expected end. The bible calls it predestined. Pre-means before, destiny means ending, so basically you see the ending before the beginning. Never be afraid to cast vision and eradicate that stinking thinking of anticipating what could go wrong and behave like its all going right. Now for my real-life example that spoke volumes to me through one of my nearest friends.

Step Three: Write Ish Down!

The list is not only for direction and discipline of keeping you on task and guiding you towards your goals, but writing the vision also is a constant reminder of what you don't want or expect. Basically, in writing the vision the prophet says to make it so big and audacious and obvious that if someone was jogging or running past it would even be clear to them that obviously you have a definite plan in motion. I remember years ago I was in the middle of a nearly million-dollar renovation project of a church that I formerly pastored in Columbus Ohio. And I shall never forget the days of different contractors showing up and the first thing they would request is to see the plans and the blueprints. Although they all had individual and, in many cases, totally different job assignments, each contractor knew that to complete the project we had to abide by the approved drawings of the architect. The plans guided us to the expected end.

My friend and Brother Ambassador Ricky Floyd in one of our many conversations over the phone one day was speaking to me about something I had going on at the time. And he inquired what was my vision before he further engaged me in conversation. I told him and he shared with me that what I was doing was not going to get me where I wanted to be on the project, and he gave me an example from his own life commentary. He told me of the time his daughter Christina was dating a guy that he didn't necessarily approve of. He mentioned how it momentarily became a source of contention between he and his only daughter. Like any father he knew that sometimes our children would do things to go against the grain or just for the sake of bucking their parents', so he tried to handle the situation with tact and taste for his daughter's happiness and his granddaughter's sake. One day things came to a head and in a heated passionate conversation his daughter asked him why didn't he approve of the young man she was dating? And his response still blows my mind to this day. He shared with her, that it wasn't that he didn't approve of the young man, but he reminded her that years prior he had his family to all write out their vision for their desired life. And he wanted her to understand as a father, nothing cheers his heart more than seeing his children happy and living a life of joy and victory. However he had no issue with the young man personally because he didn't really know the young man but he did know and reminded her that as a father he realized that the young man didn't match her vision that she had written previously. And my friend writing the vision prevents us from settling for outcomes that are less than stellar. She eventually stopped seeing the young man and last I heard was involved with a young man who matched her vision, and her father gave his nod of approval. Write the vision and make it so plain that it can be read on the run. It's tantamount to a rendering that they put on constructions sites that read coming soon. Its just to let passer byers know that there is a plan, and it is in progress.

Write your Ish down, and you'll be one step closer to getting your Ish done. See you at success.

Step Four: Bite Ish Up

"Life is Hard by the Yard, but a Sinch by the Inch"

Benjamin Elijah Mays (August 1, 1894 – March 28, 1984) was an American Baptist minister and American rights leader who is credited with laying the intellectual foundations of the American civil rights movement. Mays taught and mentored many influential activists, including Martin Luther King Jr, Julian Bond, Maynard Jackson, and Donn Clendenon, among others. His rhetoric and intellectual pursuits focused on Black self-determination. Mays' commitment to social justice through nonviolence and civil resistance were cultivated from his youth through the lessons imbibed from his parents and eldest sister. The peak of his public influence coincided with his nearly three-decade tenure as the sixth president of Morehouse College, a historically black institution of higher learning, in Atlanta, Georgia. We pause parenthetically in this moment because Reverend Mays wrote a poem that was cited in the eulogy of Dr. Martin Luther King Jr's funeral entitled "I have only just a minute."

I have only just a minute,
Only sixty seconds in it.
Forced upon me, can't refuse it.
Didn't seek it, didn't choose it.
But it's up to me.
to use it.
I must suffer if I lose it.
Give an account if I abuse it.

Just a tiny little minute,
but eternity is in it.

One of the main enemies of Reaching goals outside of Procrastination is time management. It's interesting to me the older I get; I regard time differently. I am on the lookout for time thieves daily. For the truth of the matter is when you respect time you are a person well on your way to success because you understand the urgency of now. There is no time like the present. However, you cannot do it all right now. One of the leading causes of procrastination is when a person begins to feel overwhelmed. Feeling overwhelmed and pressured by a mountainous task, anxiety takes over and usually it results in analysis paralysis. When a person overanalyzes a particular situation, they become paralyzed and, in most cases, end up not taking any action at all. This also can be attributed to overthinking.

The key to getting Ish done effectively is biting your Ish up. The adage says the one to eat an elephant is one bite at a time. I used to hear the older guys say that the way to chop down a tree is one chop at a time. I refer to an earlier section where I added that he or she who chases many rabbits catches none. Do yourself a huge favor right now and release yourself from the stress and pressure of taking on too much and overloading your plate. It's interesting to me that when I began my weight loss journey a nutritionist told me that one of the keys was to have 6 meals a day and to reduce my portion size. In other words, the frequency of my meal schedule was to charge up my metabolism, yet the flip side of our goals was that I would eventually get all my calories, it's just that I would get my calories in a way to not overwhelm my digestive system. I argue my friend that portion control is not only applicable to our physical food plates, but also our life load plates. The point as it relates to getting your Ish done is the same. You will get it done without being overwhelmed, for you will bite Ish up. Remember slow motion is better than no motion.

Lack of organization only leads to frustration.

There are so many people in the world who are not operating at their maximum potential because they have bought into the fact of this modern day thinking and mantra that says, "It is what it is." No, this mentality is totally unacceptable. If you are serious about getting your Ish done, then my friend you must get some order and some organization around your chaos. Even God Himself was organized.

Genesis 1:1-8 (KJV)
*¹ In the beginning God **created** the heaven and the earth. ² And the earth **was without form**, and void; and darkness was upon the face of the deep. And the Spirit of **God moved** upon the face of the waters. ³ And **God said**, let there be light: and there was light. ⁴ And **God saw** the light, that it was good: and **God divided** the light from the darkness. ⁵ And **God called** the light Day, and the darkness he called Night. And the evening and the morning were the first day. ⁶ And **God said,** Let there be a firmament in the midst of the waters, and **let it divide** the waters from the waters. ⁷ And **God made** the firmament, **and divided** the waters which were under the firmament from the waters which were above the firmament: and it was so. ⁸ And **God called** the firmament Heaven. And the evening and the morning were the second day.*

We've already established from the jump that I am a pastor. So, there should be no surprise by now when I refer to the bible. Someone said that an acronym for bible is Basic instructions before leaving earth. I like to say that bible stands for Be Intentional by Living Elite. Well, I take my cues from the creator. I didn't want to print the whole creation story or Genesis chapter one in its entirety, yet I wanted us to take note on how even God bit His Ish up! Look at the pattern of Gods moves when He had Ish to do.

In the beginning, lets me know that God has a sense of timing although He is an eternal now, he had a starting point. Then it says He created meaning he didn't sit around waiting on Ish to happen He made Ish happen. Also don't throw away the fact that in order to have creativity He must have had something in mind and in His head. Now although there is a theological point of something that happened between verse one and two. Which was a war, and chaos, watch Gods response. The text says there were some issues, the earth was without form, void, and also dark. And here is Gods response He moved. That's right beloved he didn't make excuses God didn't throw a pity party but rather he moved. The next thing I noticed is He moved with intention and order and strategy. He said, in so many words we can't operate when we cannot see so he started with Light. Because he needed illumination. Then there was his observation, because here we see the first benediction. Now you think of benedictions as the final words of a church service. But the word benediction is a compound word. Bene- means good, and diction- means words God looked at what he had created and put in order and celebrated the task he had completed on his things to do list. Then he divided the light from the darkness and that's organization. And he placed things in their respective places and then labeled them. Day and night, and here is God Biting Ish up. The text says the morning and the evening were the first day. I love the fact that He didn't do it all in a day although he could've. I here Christians often tout the fact that the bible says in Philippians I can do all things through Christ that strengthens me, but the flip side is that although the bible says I can do all things, doesn't mean I should do all things.

There must be order, organization and boundaries if you desire a successful end.

> *⁶ And **God said**, Let there be a firmament in the midst of the waters, and **let it divide** the waters from the waters. ⁷ And **God made** the firmament, **and divided** the waters which were under the firmament from the waters which were above the firmament: and it was so. ⁸ And **God called** the firmament Heaven. And the **evening and the morning were the second day**.*

Here's what blesses me he continued, meaning he didn't leave the job half done vs. 6 says he spoke, he separated, that's order and then he finished his day and that was the second day. And as this first chapter of the bible which is our creation narrative, progresses we see God didn't create the world in a hurry and he bit His Ish up and created the world in 6 days, one day at a time.

Therefore, if God Bit His Ish up, then certainly we ought to follow suit. Again, theologians believe that there was a war in heaven between verses 1-2 and this was the angelic fall out. Therefore verse 2 onward is an account of God rearranging the cosmos. It's where we get our word cosmetology which means to beautify and to rearrange and bring order to. Now I'm not a gambling man but I am willing to bet that when God created his angels he did not plan on the satanic fallout and having to cast rogue angels which became demons out, and then having to start again. However, it also shows us Gods ability to not only have tremendous and stellar organizational skills, but also his flexibility in His being able to pivot.

If you are going to get your Ish done, you must be flexible enough to plan well and pivot. When I say plan well, I simply mean Build for where you are going. In 2017 I attended the international Pastors and Leaders Conference in Orlando Florida hosted by Bishop Thomas Dexter Jakes Sr. ironically it was the year I first heard in person Bishop Dale Bronner. He was on to preach the noon day general assembly message. I was awestruck at his elocutionary expertise and his ability to articulate and communicate in such a loquacious way. Bisho Bronner spoke in depth about what was breaking news in March of 2017 a month before the conference. The world watched as I-85 in Atlanta Georgia collapsed and seemingly there were these random fires. He went on to explain that the fires were started by mischievous teens looking for five minutes of fame. Yet, after much deliberation and investigation they discovered the why of the freeway collapse. He says that no one expected 20 years earlier that Atlanta would become a national hotspot and mecca of sorts where everybody who was serious about relocation wanted to live in Hotlanta as it is called affectionately. And over a million people at that time had moved to the already overpopulated city. As a result, he surmised to the over 14,000 attendees that Atlanta's infrastructure could not handle its Influx. When the city planners who normally plan according to a trajectory and a projection, had no way of foreseeing that over a million plus people would move to the city in that short amount of time, and as a result the highways were not built for that amount of rigor by the large influx of vehicles daily commuting the main interstate thoroughfare. And he said the greatest lesson learned from the incident was Always build for where you are going.

Likewise in life we should plan and build for where we are going. The next lesson we learn from this genesis account of creation is that whenever you are doing anything, you must be flexible enough to pivot if necessary.

Step Four: Bite Ish Up

At the time of me penning this literary offering, I am preaching through our first series of 2024ward, about the importance of being able to PIVOT. Because biting Ish up doesn't guarantee that things will go according to plan. It just means that as we are going about accomplishing our Ish, we are aware that there may be opposition, but all our lives we have been accustomed to dealing with opposition, so we must be willing to make the necessary adjustments in the moments that we need to. I emphasize that the ability to pivot shows flexibility and separates you from those who choose to stay stuck in the mundane. Whatever you are not changing, you are choosing.

Netflix made an adjustment when blockbuster refused to change. I'm sure anyone born before 1985 can remember the great VHS tape revolution. Yes, it was 1985 when the first Blockbuster store opened in Dallas Texas renting VHS and Beta video cassette tapes. Before long the owner David Cook, who started his business because most mom-and-pop video stores only had limited inventory, had franchised nearly 8,000 store locations with more to come. At its height Block Buster had over 11,000 locations nationwide. The tragedy of this once industry giant is that a company called Netflix had the foresight of what was to come online. And all because Blockbuster refused to pivot, Netflix waited them out and came out with The Redbox idea and eventually on demand. And then purchased Blockbuster for pennies on the dollar and shut down the 11,000 stores. You rarely hear anyone mention blockbuster anymore because Netflix had the ability to Pivot.

My friend in your journey of getting Ish done, never be afraid to focus on completing one task well before taking on multiple projects at once unless life requires you to do so in that moment. Now allow me to say that yes life itself will pull you in a plethora of directions and there is nothing wrong with multi-tasking. The idea of Biting your Ish up is about organizing your life in a way as to relieve the pressure to perform and the rigor of grinding constantly to the point of exhaustion. Katy Leeson is a woman I've never met however I follow her on twitter, and she posted something that resonated in my spirit, and I want to pass it on. She says "we NEED to stop glamourizing overworking. Please. She says the absence of sleep, good, diet, exercise, relaxation, and time with friends and family isn't something to be applauded. Too many people wear their burnout as a badge of honor. And it needs to change."

Here is the point, you are not broken, there is nothing wrong with you, stop self-judging and for Gods sake get out of your head with negative self. Give yourself some grace. Stop blaming yourself for past actions, and decisions when you most likely operated from the knowledge you had available at the time. And let's make the necessary adjustments to get your Ish Done!

Step by step you can make the journey. It's about your pace, it's not about a race. Gain focus and allow yourself the wiggle room to finish well and complete each task with excellence. It's not about what you accomplish while you are getting Ish done, its about who you become in the process. I close this section with a quote I may have mentioned earlier from my aunt Martha who's gone home to be with The Lord. The card she gave me on my graduation service, read Charles Edward, always remember the largest room in the world is the room for improvement and, all of us have some room for that!

One Bite of Ish at a time PLEASE!

Step Five: Own Your Ish: Stop Playing the Blame Game!

"There is Nothing More Expensive than a Missed Opportunity."

Proverbs 28:13 (TLB)
13 A man who refuses to admit his mistakes can never be successful. But if he confesses and forsakes them, he gets another chance.

It took me years to learn that your past doesn't define you, it refines you. The word refine means to remove impurities or unwanted elements from something as part of a process. It also means to improve (something) by making small changes, in particular make (an idea, theory, or method) more subtle and accurate. The word refine is synonymous with such words like purify, clarify, clear, cleanse, sift, filter, process, improve, perfect, hone, temper, fine-tune, elaborate, touch up, revise, edit.

I used to have an administrative assistant, and one day we had a very hard conversation. The challenge first was we both were libras, and not that I am a zodiac type person who lives by horoscopes, but there is something to be said about personality traits that people born under the same sign share. At any rate I braced myself for what I thought was going to be a knock down drag out fight. However, I was shocked because when I confronted her as gentle and loving, yet firm as I could without seeming accusatory or attacking, she looked at me and uttered these words. "I can own that." Talk about being speechless, and I am never at a loss for words. But it was that day, I learned a valuable lesson. You can't fix, what you are not willing to face.

That day, rather she realized it or not she set us both free. Because if I am honest, I was not the easiest nut to crack, and I was out of order because I was self-righteous to say the least in my approach in the matter. That is why now when I have a teachable moment with people who have disputes, I ask the question; is being right more important than being kind? The reason I mentioned that she set us both free is because her owning her part in the debacle made me own up to the part I played in the matter. It is a day we both got breakthrough and grew from the experience. Thank you, Jocelyn, for stretching me and being vulnerable enough to trust in the moment that I wouldn't mismanage your humility. That was many years ago, but it is relevant to getting our Ish done, because none of us can expect to be successful if we refuse to own the stuff or admit the things about ourselves that may be some very uncomfortable truths. I have a book that will be released soon about getting into legal trouble when I was younger. The book is entitled "Felony Doesn't mean failure: I'm Not my mistake." One of the main quotes I use in the book is what Bishop T. D. Jakes said that I will never forget. He said you may have done it, but you are not it! And that's what I want to close out this section and step with, is I need for you to get that in your spirit. You are not your mistake.

You got it Honest.

Growing up with older parents you pick up a lot of older sayings that the elders used to say a lot without having to say a lot. And a lot of times if you showed a particular trait that was inherently like one of your parents or both in some cases. They would say you got it honest. Meaning you can't help but be like them because you came from them. For instance, if a person has a parent or parents that can sing extremely well, and the child has phenomenal vocal ability, they will say that child got it honest. I hate to admit it but this blame game stuff we got it honest.

The original blame game started in the garden of Eden with our original parents Adam and Eve.

Genesis 2:16-17 (KJV)
¹⁶ And the LORD God commanded the man, saying, Of every tree of the garden thou mayest freely eat: ¹⁷ But of the tree of the knowledge of good and evil, thou shalt not eat of it: for in the day that thou eatest thereof thou shalt surely die.

Genesis 3:9-14 (KJV)
⁹ And the LORD God called unto Adam, and said unto him, Where art thou? ¹⁰ And he said, I heard thy voice in the garden, and I was afraid, because I was naked; and I hid myself. ¹¹ And he said, Who told thee that thou wast naked? **Hast thou eaten of the tree,** *whereof I commanded thee that thou shouldest not eat? ¹² And* **the man said, The woman whom thou gavest** *to be with me,* **she gave me** *of the tree, and I did eat. ¹³ And the LORD* **God said unto the woman, What is this that thou hast done?** *And* **the woman said, The serpent beguiled me,** *and I did eat. ¹⁴ And the LORD God said unto the serpent, Because thou hast done this, thou art cursed above all cattle, and above every beast of the field; upon thy belly shalt thou go, and dust shalt thou eat all the days of thy life:*

Do you see the progression of the passage as it unfolds into a blame game? Adam blamed Eve and she blamed the serpent. A classical case of what A character played by the late actor Flip Wilson who played a character in a skit named Geraldine; and whenever confronted about an unscrupulous act or behavior he would say "the devil made me do it." The unfortunate truth is the devil can't make us do anything. The enemy only plants seed in our mind, and we normally carry out the deed. The point is still replete, blaming someone else does not obliterate the fact that error, or an infraction was committed. One of the ways we can get over this character hurdle is to understand that just because it's factual, does not mean its final. There is grace available when we just like Jocelyn did "own it."

1 John 1:8-9 (KJV)
*⁸ If we say that we have no sin, we deceive ourselves, and the truth is not in us. ⁹ **If we confess** our sins, **he is faithful and just to forgive us** our sins, **and to cleanse us from all** unrighteousness.*

Let's just all own our bad ish (issues, sins, and hard hearts) so that we can move forward to our more important Ish (intentional, strategic, habits). Because remember We got Ish to do. And because he handled it for us, we are free because of calvaries complete work, to move in our purpose unincumbered by the pass. Just own it so we can move on!

Colossians 2:14 (TLB)
¹⁴ and blotted out the charges proved against you, the list of his commandments which you had not obeyed. He took this list of sins and destroyed it by nailing it to Christ's cross.

No excuse NICK.

Your only competition is the person in the mirror. I learned this lesson from a book I read about a man born with no limbs named

Nick Vujicic. He was born with no arms and no legs. He wrote a book in 2012 entitled "Living Above Your Circumstances: your life without limits." He's travelled the world encouraging millions of people to overcome adversity with faith, hope, love, and courage so that they may pursue their dreams. Without any limbs he is a father, husband, best-selling author, and his message teaches that all of us have adversity, some may be unique, but mostly all are universal. My point for bringing up Mr. Vujicic is two-fold. For if he can go around the world with no arms and no legs and not allow his being limbless not make him limitless then what's our excuse who are well abled. He mentioned how he must wait for someone to give him a drink of water because he can't hold a cup, as well as other things that his caretaker and family do for him that the average person takes for granted, yet he's grateful for even the small things. The second reason I bring him up is because he owns his Ish, boldly, unashamedly, and most of all unapologetically. He embraced his challenges and decided that if he had breath in his torso, he would do the best he could to find Gods will for his life. He capstones his journey for living a life void of excuses this way. He says if you put the word go in front of the word disable it spells GODISABLE!

Excuse me I'm in my own way.

When you want to do something, you find a way, when you don't want to do a thing, you find an excuse. Now that you have owned your Ish. You realize that excuses must be eliminated. It is also my hope that through this body of work, you have not just consumed valuable information, but also utilized some real time application. The ultimate breakthrough will come when you own your Ish to the point that you want to succeed in getting Ish done, as much as you want to breathe. It is in that moment where you are liberated because you then fully embrace the challenges and opposition, not as enemies but employees working for your good.

Your Struggles are your Strength.

A young boy who was born without a left arm was sent to Judo lessons by his mother in a bid to help with his confidence. So, he began taking lessons with an old Japanese master.

Every practice session the master taught the boy one throw. Just one technique over and over again.

Ever so often the one-armed boy would see the other students learning different techniques and ask the master why he wasn't learning anything else.

The master always replied – "Just focus on this one throw. Keep practicing"

Several months later, it was the state Judo championships and the old master entered the young boy.

The young boy was terrified.

The first match began, and the one-armed boy grabbed his opponent and to the shock of all the spectators – easily flipped him to the ground. Instant win!

The second round was a little harder, but the one-armed boy again pulled off the technique – the only technique he knew and won.

The third and fourth round amazingly went the same way and the young boy found himself in the tournament final facing a much bigger, stronger, and tougher opponent, who had won the tournament for three straight years.

The young boy was overmatched it seemed. The referee and the organizers of the tournament spoke to the master and asked him if he wanted to withdraw his student..

"No" said the master. "We will fight".

As the final match began the entire crowd were on the edge of their seat. The opponent stepped and grabbed the young one-armed boy and pulled him towards him. For a second it looked as if it was all over...

But then the one-armed boy reached with his right hand, stepped in and BOOM – he threw his opponent flat on his back, to win the match!

The crowd went nuts – the one-armed boy was the state Judo Champion!

On the drive home, the young boy asked his teacher – "Was this a set-up? Did they just let me win because I only have one arm? I only know one technique – these guys know hundreds!"

The teacher replied "No – you won fair and square. But there are two reasons. You won because you mastered one of the most devastating techniques in Judo. And the only known way to defend against that throw is to grab the left arm!" And because you don't have one it is impossible to defend against you when using that technique. What appeared to be an incredible weakness – was in fact his greatest strength?

Get up and get your Ish Done! It's beyond Time.

The following commandments are taught in the master class coaching tool that we highly recommend for those who want to invest in maximizing the skills necessary for becoming a master distraction and procrastination eliminator.

The Ten Commandments of Being Intentional
1. **Thou Shalt Use Your Thumbs**
2. **Thou Shalt Stop Wishing For it and Start Working for It!**
3. **Thou Shalt Get out of Thine Own Way**

4. Thou shalt not Keep Using Excuses
5. Thou shalt be about it and Stop talking about it
6. Thou Shalt Shift Thine Thinking
7. Thou Shalt Make History Not Repeat it
8. Thou Shalt not Live in Fear
9. Thou Shalt Change Your Expectation Level
10. Thou Shalt Get ISH Done

Bonus:

The ten commandments of Getting Ish Done
The group coaching for $9,997 (reg. ~~$19,997~~) includes:
Masterminds retreat a 2 day one on one intensive with Charles Bond
Master class covering: Top 3 getting Ish Done killers hands down.
Mindset
Misaligned loyalty
Mal adjusted time management.

In which I'll do in depth teaching on each step and go deeper into the principles for you to yield maximum results.

Bonus Round for Believers Who Are Serious About Understanding from A Biblical Narrative the Journey to Getting Ish Done Life Lessons.

Getting ISH Done

Why Did God Give Me Another Year?

Luke 13:6-9 (KJV)
⁶ He spake also this parable; A certain man had a fig tree planted in his vineyard; and he came and sought fruit thereon, and found none. ⁷ Then said he unto the dresser of his vineyard, Behold, these three years I come seeking fruit on this fig tree, and find none: cut it down; why cumbereth it the ground? ⁸ And he answering said unto him, Lord, let it alone this year also, till I shall dig about it, and dung it: ⁹ And if it bear fruit, well: and if not, then after that thou shalt cut it down.

I often wonder when I really take time to look over my life. Out of all the things that I done, some good and some bad. I can admit that I've known some people who were better by accident than I was on purpose. And here it is they are dead and gone, and yet here I am still alive. It makes me ask, why did God give me another year?

When I look at all the tragedies, we've witnessed over the past 3-5 years. Like hurricane Dorian took out the entire island of the Bahamas killing several people. If you remember Hawaii had massive fires destroying many homes leaving many dead. In Dayton OH a gunman went into Walmart and randomly killed nine people and injured 27 more. In Buffalo NY a racist went inside of a grocery store and open fire with the automatic weapon killing any black person in sight. I'm sure many of you remember in Uvalde TX a young man went into an elementary school took the lives of innocent children and teachers for no known reason.

It makes me wonder Lord why would you give me another year?

And my brothers and sisters as I was pondering the tragedies of this year and years past. I began not only to think in retrospection, but with introspection and I wanted to know out of all of the lives gone some in mere innocence, some in their youth. Why is it that I was not one of them. WHY is it that you and I didn't pass on in our sleep? Why is it that every day we ride the dangerous highways and byways interstates and roads of our individual cities, why is it that in these transitional moments didn't we transition? Why is it that in spite of conflict, challenge and potential catastrophic calamity, everyday God has spared our lives and now here we are in another year.

Now allow me to stop and remind you before you answer that question in your mind, that it was not because of something that we have done so good. No not at all, and it's not because we made all the right decisions. And the only answer I could come up with was, God perhaps gave us another year because there was possibly something he was trying to do in our life with our life and through our lives that required an extension.

So such is the case in our text. Jesus here in his pedagogical style of preaching, and teaching tells us a parable. Parabolos in Latin is two words, para meaning to come along side of, and bolos meaning to throw. Jesus taught in parables for 3 reasons. First, because they were portable, meaning you could carry them with you. Secondly, they were simple, even a child could comprehend. But thirdly, because they were universal, in that they were earthly stories with heavenly meanings that Jesus would throw alongside of his teachings to give us as believers some JOY FOR OUR JOURNEY!

It talks about a man who had planted a vineyard, and he hired a dresser, gardener, or a manager to keep the vineyard while he was away. After a while the owner came by to check with the steward about the progress and productivity of the crop. He noticed that one of the trees had not produced in three years. The owner thought about the capital he had lost, and he said to the dresser, look get your axe and cut this tree down. I've spent money on it, and now it's affecting my capital and my productivity. Get rid of it because it's taking up space. And the manager said Sir, wait a minute. I know that you're upset, I know that you're angry. But give me 52 more weeks, give me 12 more months, give me 365 more days, give me:

8,760 more hours with it
525,600 more minutes with it
31,536,000 more seconds with it.

Give me one more year with the tree. And if it's not where you want it to be when you come back, I'll get rid of it and cut it down.

Sis and Bros this is not just some antiquated parable. But in this parable, many believe the hermeneutic refers to the condition of the children of Israel. I believe that it's really talking about you and I. Because the Owner of the Vineyard represents God, the manager or the dresser represents Jesus, and the tree represents you and me. The three years are representative of the existential purpose and meaning of why we still don't know who we are, how we got here, and where we are going.

And if God came back today and said to the dresser cut it down. I yet still hear Jesus saying God please give them one more year!

That's why we ought to be thanking God, and praising God like we have lost our minds. Like we have gone coo-coo for coco puffs. That's why we ought to be grateful instead of hateful. That's why we ought to raise a praise voluntarily, because when we should have been cut down, Jesus said, God give them one more year.

So, I need to know from God why is it that you've given us another year?

Number one, he gave us another year so that we can be **FORGIVEN**.

He says right there in vs 8. Lord let it alone, that phrase literally means aphomi in the Greek meaning give it another opportunity.

In your justice you could get rid of it, says the vine dresser. But Lord I'm not appealing to your justice, I'm appealing to your mercy. There's some stuff they need to get rid of GOD let them alone.

One more year so they can get their business straight and somebody here, you're holding a grudge and been holding it against someone for 5 years, you need to let it go the old folks used to say we are living on borrowed time let it go if she was supposed to marry you in 1995 and she married freaky Freddy get over it, if he stole her she wasn't yours in the beginning, if he was supposed to be your man and he left you for another woman, honey let it go. God forgives you predicated on how you forgive others no wonder he said in that model prayer of Matt:6 forgive us our trespasses as we not if we forgive those who trespass against us and reason why is if you not forgiving folks because they lied on you, you need to think about how you done lied on some folks. Life is like a boomerang, what goes around comes around. So, he gives us another year #1 so we can be forgiven. All of us have some things we need to be forgiven for, and from. We are operating on what the late Pastor E.L. McKinney called the "I haven't lately" system.

I can't say I have never stolen; I just haven't stolen anything lately.

I can't say I have never lied; I just can say I haven't lied lately.

I can't say I have never fornicated; I just haven't fornicated lately.

Touch two people and tell them to join the club.

Secondly, he gives us another year, so that we can be **FIXED**.

The gardener said Lord, give me another year so that I can dig around it. Which literally means God there are some weeds around it that is prohibiting and preventing it from growing. So, God let me fix on it, and get rid of whatever weeds that are preventing it from growth. Let me (parenthetically pause) to ask you a question and it's a self-test so grade your own paper. What habits are your weeds? Or are you too busy, indulging in unproductive vices, like gateway drugs such as marijuana. And maybe God gave you another year so he can de-weed you from weed. And if that's a bit extreme; maybe your habit is the lottery, or the casino, or promiscuity, your weed maybe scratch offs; or some man you are head over hill about. Or is that girl that works with you that always wear the little miniskirt and meet you at the water cooler for break; or is gossiping and lying on folks your weed. The point is all of us could use some pruning and weed pulling in our lives.

He says let me give you another year so I can get rid of some weeds. He says I want to forgive you. I want to fix you. But finally, and thirdly he gives us another year so he can **FERTILIZE** us.

Lord let me dig-that's fixing but also let me dung it that's the fertilizing; that word literally in the Greek means; let me put some Manure around you; let me put some fecal matter around you. Let me put some MESS let me put some (as the little kids used to say) BOO BOO. Let me put some mess around the trees, because there are nutrients inside the manure that produce maximum growth.

And I had to wonder because it bothered me theologically JESUS why would you put mess, and manure around the tree? He says Bond don't you understand fertilization, you're from the country the best fertilizing entity is manure, and although it smells bad, it's still a strength builder because it makes stuff grow.

Has anybody here ever been through some mess that you thought was going to take you out, but it took you up?

God is saying you ought to give me praise for your mess. And somebody you've had to learn how to maneuver through some manure, but you found out it was a blessing in your messing, so you weren't going through you were growing through.

So, what I thought was going to destroy me was sent to develop me. I'm closing the book but really God my contamination was really the motivation for my gratification. Because if I never had a problem, how would I know God could solve them? Lord instead of complaining I used to hear my old daddy say thank God, that things are as well as they are. I didn't deserve to be here, but I thank God that when I should have been cut down; he protected me, he planted me, and then he pruned me. I was sinking deep in sin far from a peaceful shore. I was very stained within sinking to rise no more. Then the master of the sea heard my despairing cry, and from the waters lifted me, now safe am I. Love lifted me. love lifted me when nothing else could help love lifted. I close with a story of two insurance men who attended a conference every year in this particular city. And the only option for food was a Diner across from the convention hall. They hated going there because the service was horrible, it wasn't the cleanest facility, however by it being a small town with no big brand restaurants, it was the only cooked food available outside of vending machines. They would go there year after year. One day while there attending the conference they went across the street to grab some lunch on their break before the crowd would get in. And when they walked in, they were greeted by a well-dressed host. They were seated at a clean table with fresh table linen. The waitress that took their order had a winsome smile and winning attitude and personality. And for some reason the food was delicious, as though it had been prepared by a top-class chef. They asked to see a manager because they were confused and wanted to know if this was the same restaurant, they had eaten at years prior? And the manager replied yes it was the same restaurant. Then the manager asked them did they read the sign when they walked in, they both answered no. he advised them to go out and read the sign. They went out and came back in and said yes you were right, the sign confirmed that it was the same restaurant they had eaten at in previous years. But the manager asked them to go back and read the sign above the restaurant name sign. They both went out and instantly noticed what the drastic changes were a result of. The sign read the same restaurant but UNDER NEW MANAGEMENT! That's our testimony my friend we are still inherently the same person we were physically and otherwise. However, the difference is when Christ is in the equation, the difference is we are under new management. Thak God it's a New Year and a New you and I. Thank God for another year. Years ago, Mr. Walter Hawkins put out a song that said Thak you Lord for all you've done for me! The lyrics are my sentiment:

Tragedies are commonplace, all kinds of diseases, people are slipping away. The economy is down, people can't get enough pay, but as for me, all I can say is. Thank you, Lord, for all You've done for me, yeah, Folks without homes, living out in the streets, And the drug habits some say, they just can't beat. Muggers and robbers, no place seems to be safe, But You'll be my protection every step of the way, And I want to say is, Thank you Lord for all You've done for me, yeah, It could have been me (thank you) Outdoors (thank you), No food (thank you), No clothes (thank you) Or left alone (thank you), Without a friend (thank you),Or just another number (thank you) With a tragic end (thank you)But you didn't see fit to let none of these things be (thank you), Cause everyday by your power you keep on keeping me. And I just want to say Thank you Lord for all you've done for me.

2019 was a rough year. But I still after burying my last living brother, going through a second divorce, and then burying my father all in one year within 8 months. I still say thank you Lord for all you've done for me.

Getting ISH Done

7 Distinctions to Being an Extraordinary HUMAN!

Foundation:

1. **Integrity** - Honor your word as yourself. That is do what you said you would do by when you said you would do it. And when you don't clean it up make new promises and keep them. Be impeccable with your word.

2. **Being Racket Free** - Give up Being right, even when you know you are right) get off it before others know you are on it. Then stop allowing rackets around you. Remember being kind is more important than just being hellbent on being right.

3. **Being Powerful** - Be straight in your communication and take what you get. Real power is when you can create real results with communication, for when you choose power by force you have to use coercion and manipulation.

4. **Be Courageous** - acknowledge your fear and then act. 2nd Timothy 1:7 For God has not given us the spirit of fear; but of power, and of love, and of a sound mind.

5. **Being Peaceful** - Give up the interpretation that there is something wrong. (peaceful people deal with what is so) Faith is a solid trust in God. I anticipate what can go right not what can go wrong.

6. **Being Charismatic** - give up in order to and trying to get somewhere. Just say what there is to say. Be who you are

and fully doing what you do while doing it (it is a function of presence.

7. **Being Present** - not just in body, but also in heart mind and soul. Rely on the fact of knowing God is in you.

Become A Master of Maximizing Your Time

Some Simple Truths

1. You cannot <u>create</u> more time, but you can create more value for your time and of your time.
2. We all have the <u>same</u> amount of time in one day, but we don't have the same <u>value</u> of that time.
3. <u>Steward</u> the gift of <u>the time</u> that God gave to all of us, just like we steward his money.
4. Look in your checkbook. How you <u>steward/ spend</u> your <u>money</u> is an indication of how you <u>steward/spend</u> your time.
5. What you do not value neither will <u>anyone else</u>. And there is always someone available who will!
6. Don't become the <u>expert in</u> someone else's time, and do not <u>minimize/undervalue</u> your time by <u>spending</u> more <u>time</u> helping them
master their time.
7. Most successful people are experts at maximizing their time. They know that wasted and unproductive time takes away from success, promotion and increase because it produces nothing.
8. There is a difference between Managed time and Maximized time.
9. Managed time is for people with modest/average goals.

10. If you want true success and more money, you must join the ranks of those who have maximized time, and not just managed time.

Getting Your ISH done means your habits allow you to thrive on purpose.

Clarity on the OUTCOME

1. What do you really want? (not what does someone else think you should do, have or be - what do YOU want?)
2. Is this goal something that can be initiated and maintained by you? If not, think of something that YOU can initiate and maintain. For example, you may want your spouse to listen to you, it may even be a goal of yours. But you cannot initiate and control that. You can change the way you communicate to improve the chances of that happening, but you cannot initiate or maintain his listening.
3. Is this goal stated positively? If not, take a minute to state it in the positive sense. For example, "I want to enter college and complete my bachelor's degree." Rather than, "My goal is to not be stuck in this job anymore." When the goal is in our control and stated positively, the brain suddenly can organize behavior to start making things happen. In the example, the brain may start listing out tasks like look up the requirements online, compare those to your experience and education, create a gap analysis and start looking for opportunities and ways to fill the gaps - which suddenly starts narrowing us down on what we say YES to!!!! Whereas when it is not in our control or stated positively, the brain does not move towards a solution you really want.

If you just do not want to be at this job anymore, a solution may be to quit and find a new one, but that may be more of the same, or worse.

4. In what context do you want this goal? That means, where, when, and with whom do you want this goal? If I had a goal of being happy "all the time" and found a way to program that in, I may run into trouble at the next funeral I go to. I would have overgeneralized "happy." So, where, when, and with whom do you want this outcome? Be specific and consider how achieving your result will impact other areas and people in your life.

5. What measurable and quantifiable evidence will you have that you have achieved your goal?

Specifically, what will you see, hear, and feel when you have achieved your goal? We are often guilty of not stopping to smell the roses...there is a song that really clearly points out, "I wish somebody would have told me that someday these will be the good ole days..." If we don't know what we want or what it looks and feels like, we may miss that we actually arrived and have it!! Take a minute to actually visualize and hear and feel what will be going on for you in the future when you have what you really want and write it down!

6. What are the positives in your life/situation right now as is?

7. How can you build those existing positives into your future life / situation / new outcome?

8. If you really had what you wanted - your desired outcome - in a meaningful way, what would having that get for you? And if you REALLY had that new outcome, you just came up with, what would really having that get for you that is more important than all of that? And if you had this new

outcome in a meaningful way, what would having that allow you to do or have or be that is bigger than all of that? This is very important to understand your motivation for going for it.

9. What resources do you have and what resources do you need to help you get what you really want?
10. What are the first or next SMALL steps to start moving towards what you really want? Make sure this is a manageable step! Consider several options for getting started and pick the one that makes the most sense for where you are in your life right now?
11. When will you take that first small step?

CLARITY ON WHAT IS AT STAKE

12. Make a mental movie of you in the future having fully achieved EVERYTHING you REALLY want as if it were true. Look at how your days go and how your life is. Notice how different you are. Notice how it feels to have achieved what you really want. Notice how you have the things you really want - THIS IS WHAT IS AT STAKE FOR YOU - and your limiting beliefs are the things that are holding you back from having all of this.
13. Now shake that off and look at a movie of your life at that exact same point in time that you just saw...except see yourself clinging to your old beliefs and patterns having CHANGED NOTHING. Notice how you look, and how you feel.
14. Now see yourself 5 years from there still clinging to your old beliefs and patterns, still having changed nothing. Notice how you look, how you feel, and what your life

looks like. This is the life your limiting beliefs will allow you to continue to create. Frustrated. Stuck. Wanting more. Knowing you should. But knowing you cannot continue doing the same things and expect a different result, my friend this is called insanity.

15. Having seen this and knowing what is at stake for you now, what does this make possible for you NOW?
16. What new behaviors are you willing to try? What new experiences are you willing to create?

Show me what you are working with!

2 Kings 4:1-7 (KJV)
¹ Now there cried a certain woman of the wives of the sons of the prophets unto Elisha, saying, Thy servant my husband is dead; and thou knowest that thy servant did fear the Lord: and the creditor is come to take unto him my two sons to be bondmen.
² And Elisha said unto her, What shall I do for thee? Tell me, what hast thou in the house? And she said, Thine handmaid hath not any thing in the house, save a pot of oil.
³ Then he said, Go, borrow thee vessels abroad of all thy neighbours, even empty vessels; borrow not a few.
⁴ And when thou art come in, thou shalt shut the door upon thee and upon thy sons, and shalt pour out into all those vessels, and thou shalt set aside that which is full.
⁵ So she went from him, and shut the door upon her and upon her sons, who brought the vessels to her; and she poured out.

⁶ And it came to pass, when the vessels were full, that she said unto her son, Bring me yet a vessel. And he said unto her, there is not a vessel more. And the oil stayed.
⁷ Then she came and told the man of God. And he said, Go sell the oil, and pay thy debt, and live thou and thy children the rest.

The blaring theme of this passage is not evident at first glance. Because when we jaywalk in this scriptural neighborhood, we are hit head on with devastation. Here is a woman whose husband has transitioned unexpected. To make matters worse, he obviously leaves her in a predicament that jeopardizes her son's freedom and future due to the societal laws on debt. Her credit cards are maxed out. Her hope is defeated and she goes to the one place that she sought relief, she goes where most people go when they've exhausted their other options. She goes to church. My assignment is perspective, for if I am completely honest it took me years to come into the realization that its not what life throws at us that determines our destiny, but rather how we respond to what life throws our way. Its all about perspective.

Now don't misinterpret what I am saying. I am not suggesting that life will not throw some devastating blows, nor am I saying that every time we are hit we should develop a Teflon exterior and like the old timex watches take a licking and keep on ticking, as though nothing happens. What I am saying is that when life knocks us to our knees and it will. We cannot afford to stay stuck at what was a temporary time stamp. Never put a period where God put a comma, because I do not tell people in storms to build a bridge and get over it. I just say you may never get over it, but for the sake of destiny you have to learn to get past it.

And this my friend requires perspective. It is in moments like this that we learn your outlook determines your outcome. Perspective is the difference between what you lost and what you have left. The enemy will have your perspective so discombobulated that you will be so hurt over what you have lost, until you will not be able to fathom what can be, thus you lose sight of what you still have left. And if he can keep you disgruntled and thrown off, he distracts us with what was. When you become distracted you become defeated.

I do not blame her for being human and feeling the mournful gut-wrenching blow of the devastation that death brings especially when its unexpected. But I do charge her with not at least being spiritual enough to trust in the God of her salvation. I hear you saying, now pastor why would you question her spirituality? Because being spiritual does not always guarantee that one will be strong and strategic. Yet when I read the passage from a more easier said than done purview, I learn that she was married to a prophet and my challenge is how can you be that close to the anointing and that close to the word and not at least be able to say God I trust you even when I can't trace you.

You see I understand we all respond differently to disaster, but tragedy will sometimes reveal if you were a person of God, or if you trust the personification of God. All that means is many cases you have to not only trust God even if you can't trace him, but even when all hell breaks loose and it don't all make sense, you have a relationship with God that says I at least trust that my God will make sense of it all.

Cry if you must, grieve at your own pace, go through the borage of emotions, but still rise and say like Job though you slay me yet will I trust you. Again, you may never get over It, but you must get past it.

One philosophical poet said it this way:

Like is like a camera: Focus on what's important, Capture the good times, develop from the negatives, and if things do not work out, take another shot.

YOUR CONDITION SHOULDN'T CHANGE YOUR CONFESSION OR YOUR CONVICTIONS

When the prophet asked her what was wrong, she insisted on all the negatives that she could not see that she was stating what is a known behavior called being obsessed with the obvious.

Years ago, a young man was drafted into the military. It was brought to the attention of his commanding officers that he had a keen ability to train and work with dogs. They assigned him to the k-9 unit where his assignment was to train dogs to detect bombs. For this to be successful he would have to spend a long uninterrupted period of time with these dogs. one day after having a long record of training several successful bombs detecting k-9's, he was assigned another one and his stint would normally be 16 months of constant, contact with the dogs. he was assigned a German shepherd and day in and day out as it was his custom he collaborated with this dog. He received a call to go on leave for his wife had given birth so their first-born baby, however the mother did not survive giving birth and died after having the baby. His superiors thought that it would be good to send the dog home with him because he would be on leave for a lengthy period, and he had already spent 13 months with the dog it just didn't make sense for them to break up the duo and it would probably give the soldier some company to assist in his grieving process while he became accustomed to being a single father and caring for a new born.

It became custom that everywhere the man went the dog, and the baby were right by his side. If you saw one you saw all three. One day the man needed to go up the road to a neighbor's house that was in earshot his home which set on the edge of a wooded area in the rural. He left the baby sleeping in the bassinet and the left the dog there on guard. He was gone for 10 minutes and when he returned, he was not prepared for what he found. He walked through the front door and the furniture was disorganized as though a tsunami had ripped through his living room. He walked back to the bedroom and was flabbergasted. The dog was laying there in front of the turned over bassinet with blood running down his mouth. There was no sign of the baby, and he traced the line of blood out of the bedroom don't the hall out of the front do over toward the woods. Devastated he went in the house grabbed the shotgun from behind the door and shot the dog. After the shot rang out, he hears a faint cry from behind the dresser. He looked behind the dresser and right there was his little baby alive and well. But how could it be? All the evidence pointed to the fact that apparently the dog had a fit of rage and ate the baby or killed it and dragged it to the edge of the woods. He followed the trail of blood this time over to the edge of the woods and there he discovered the truth. He saw lying there a dead wolf.

The man was guilty of being obsessed with the obvious. He discovered what happened while he was away because he had left the door ajar, a wolf came in and obviously tried to get the baby. Apparently, the dog to defend the baby fought with the wolf and killed the wolf. Afterwards he dragged the wolfs lifeless body to the edge of the woods and left it there. Went back to the house and turned over the bassinet and put the baby in the blanket over behind the dresser and lay there until his master returned. His baby was alive, but he killed his companion dog, because he was obsessed with the obvious. He was enamored with the fact that he assumed at first glance the worst and not what was possible.

She never took time to see that even when my situation does not reflect my expectations of life, that God can still get Glory out of your story if you keep your belief in the face of grief.

A bend in the road ain't the end of the road because, God is the only person I know who will take you through a tragedy to make you a trophy.

Here's your something to shout about.

YOUR PURPOSE IS ALWAYS BIGGER THAN YOUR PROBLEM

However, that's when you need to surround yourself with voices that can show you victory, outside of your victimization.

Elijah was not in denial of her dilemma but rather he understood that just because its factual does not mean its final.

Yes, her husband died, that's a fact. Yes, he left her in debt, that's a fact. Yes, the creditors were threatening to take her sons as indentured servants, that's a fact.

However, God is still in control, and even when a thing is over our heads, it is still under his feet. I invite your attention away from her disastrous dilemma and let's look at the dialogue from the prophet.

The prophet makes a strange inquiry "what's in your house?" Not, because he was being insensitive but in the face of failure you need someone who's in touch with God who can reveal to you that OBSTACLES ARE OPPORTUNITIES TURNED INSIDE OUT.

PROBLEMS ARE OPPORTUNITIES IN WORK CLOTHES

She said all I have is some oil. That's the game changer in the passage because if oil is all you have, with God on your side Oil is all you need. Now for your non-bible readers, oil don't sound like much. This is why you must look at her culture.

In her culture oil was an asset and commodity. Because in every house you went into, in those days, by the door were two items, a wash pot and a cruise or bottle of oil.

There was a wash pot because the roads were dusty, and when you went into a person's house, a servant would wash your feet, secondly, they would take oil mixed with fragrance and anoint your head and your feet with oil to refresh you from your journey. Take note beloved this happened in everybody's house. Therefore, if everybody used oil, everybody needs oil. Yall didn't get it so let me say it slow, so I can say it some more.

If everyone used oil, then that meant every household had a need for oil. Now those of you who are intuitive the least bit can already discern that it looked like a little because of her lens. Because it's hard to be optimistic when you have a misty optic. But the fact that she had some oil once put into perspective by someone who looks at things through God like glasses. She was in the right place for the prophet to tell her that oil is not insignificant, she just needed instructions and inspiration.

The prophet says to her go borrow many vessels it's interesting to me that she was already in debt and now the pastor tells her to go get into some more debt. Not only that but he said go borrow many vessels from your neighbors I have an issue with that because neighbors are nosy. Then look at the instructions he continues to give. Get your sons and then close the door. It's as if he's saying to her what you thought was a burden all you needed was a business plan. And this is an opportunity to train your children how to be entrepreneurs which will affect emerging generations to come and let them know not to fall into the grips of capitalism and consumerism. Would rather teach your sons how to be creators instead of just consumers by doing so they will learn that they don't have to settle for slavery and that they can be producers instead of falling into poverty.

She says all I have is some oil but my friend that was something the God could work with. Because God always gives you something to work with. Remember oil was in high demand. When I was younger, I used to like rap music. And allow me to go further and say old school rap music there was a rapper named biz Marquis that had a song out that said ohh baby you got what I need you say he's just a friend you say he's just a friend ohh baby you got what I need. Although that seems comical the lyrics epitomize the fact that she had something that everybody needed, which was oil.

I told you God gave everyone something to work with. He gave Bill Gates Microsoft. He gave Steve Jobs apple. He gave Michael Jordan and LeBron James a basketball. He gave Colonel Sanders 14 spices and Kentucky fried chicken. He gave famous Amos a cookie recipe. He gave Oprah Winfrey A journalism degree. He gave Martin Luther King a dream. He gave Tyler Perry Madea. He gave David a slingshot, he gave Michael Jackson the moonwalk. He gave his son a cross. God gave everyone something to work with.

So, what's your excuse? I need you to look at what you have in the house. And show me what you are working with.

And he told her oil go in private with your boys shut the door and pour out.

In other words, whatever you got left God can use that and turn your whole situation around.

That's the economics, but there is also the eternal aspect. Every time you see oil in the bible, it's also representative of the anointing.

What she was really saying is not only the fact, all I have left is some oil. Really what she meant was, all I have left is my ANOINTING.

I need you to stop right now and have a moment of gratitude for the fact that you may have lost some stuff, you may have lost some friends, you may have lost some money, you may have lost some loved ones, but you still got your oil and you still got your anointing.

Where are all of the greasy oily people at that can take a moment and acknowledge that yes you have had times where you were broke busted and disgusted. Yes you've had seasons when life had tossed you around and beat you up but you still got your oil which means you still got your anointing. Can you just open your mouth right now and declare I still got oil. They took the job but they didn't take your oil. They plotted against you but you still got your anointing. They dug ditches for you and set traps for you but you still got your oil. Somebody ought to just yell to the top of your lungs I'm still oily.

Matter of fact the rest of your life is going to be the best of your life because you still got some oil left. Someone needs to acknowledge the fact that when you're down to nothing God is up to something.

Now here is the miracle. When she began to pour out on her end God was in heaven pouring out on his end. You see it was a miracle not a magic trick. A miracle is defined by doctor Donald Parsons as whenever God suspends the natural order of things.

God was in heaven pouring out on his end in other words to some it look like her life was at rock bottom but God still had one more move. As a matter of fact I heard the old country western song that said in the lyrics quote being on rock bottom is not a bad place to be because when you hit rock bottom at least you're on a rock that cannot roll.

The late Dr. Charles Booth from Columbus Ohio invited me to preach one Sunday morning at the great Olivet Baptist Church, because he was going to preach that after noon for Bishop Jerome ross. I went to hear him preach, and he told a German story called diesphelcher or better known as "Checkmate." Which is about that famous museum in Paris France called the Louvre. And in the museum is a famous

painting called Checkmate. Well in the painting it's the Devil on one side of the chess board playing a Peasant for his soul. The painting showed the devil had won the game of chess and called CHECKMATE. However, one day a young chess player visiting the museum studied the painting for hours, because something didn't look quite right. So, he stared all day fixated on the painting because all though it looks like the devil had won and declared CHECKMATE the young man just couldn't shake the fact that something just didn't seem right. As they were about to close the museum for the day the security guard was walking toward him to tell him that he had to leave and suddenly, he started screaming and pointing at the picture saying.

IT'S A LIE, IT'S A LIE, IT'S A LIE

They tried to calm him down and finally the managers came out and the police were called, and he kept screaming it was a lie. Finally, they asked why he was saying the painting was a lie? He said because the devil declared check, but the man he's playing has a king, and the king has got one more move.

I came by here to tell someone no matter what the enemy tried to do to you THE KING STILL GOT ONE More Move. Now show me what you are working with.

God And a Slim Chance

Judges 7:1-7 (KJV)
¹ Then Jerubbaal, who is Gideon, and all the people that were with him, rose up early, and pitched beside the well of Harod: so that the host of the Midianites were on the north side of them, by the hill of Moreh, in the valley.
² And the LORD said unto Gideon, The people that are with thee are too many for me to give the Midianites into their hands, lest Israel vaunt themselves against me, saying, Mine own hand hath saved me.
³ Now therefore go to, proclaim in the ears of the people, saying, Whosoever is fearful and afraid, let him return and depart early from mount Gilead. And there returned of the people twenty and two thousand; and there remained ten thousand.
⁴ And the LORD said unto Gideon, The people are yet too many; bring them down unto the water, and I will try them for thee there: and it shall be, that of whom I say unto thee, This shall go with thee, the same shall go with thee; and of whomsoever I say unto thee, This shall not go with thee, the same shall not go.
⁵ So he brought down the people unto the water: and the LORD said unto Gideon, Every one that lappeth of the water with his tongue, as a dog lappeth, him shalt thou set by himself; likewise every one that boweth down upon his knees to drink.

⁶ And the number of them that lapped, putting their hand to their mouth, were three hundred men: but all the rest of the people bowed down upon their knees to drink water.
⁷ And the LORD said unto Gideon, By the three hundred men that lapped will I save you, and deliver the Midianites into thine hand: and let all the other people go every man unto his place.

Judges 7:16-18 (KJV)
¹⁶ And he divided the three hundred men into three companies, and he put a trumpet in every man's hand, with empty pitchers, and lamps within the pitchers.
¹⁷ And he said unto them, Look on me, and do likewise: and, behold, when I come to the outside of the camp, it shall be that, as I do, so shall ye do.
¹⁸ When I blow with a trumpet, I and all that are with me, then blow ye the trumpets also on every side of all the camp, and say, The sword of the LORD, and of Gideon.

My brothers and sisters in 2022 while we were immersed in covid 19, overwhelmed with developing protocols, and in line for the vaccine, something historical took place at the 148th Kentucky derby in Church hill downs. An 80-1 Longshot named Rich Strike who was an alternate and got in at the last minute was a longshot and won against all odds in 2022. God will take you and me. Like Gideon as someone who wasn't even invited and not only move someone out the way, and open a spot for you, but also allow you to win.

He'll Take the Foolish Things of The World to Confound the Wise

We've been called together and chosen together and now we are collaborating. God tells Gideon that although you are facing the Midianites 100,000 plus army and you don't have but 32,000 you have too many and I can imagine Gideon thinking maybe God failed math or his calculator is broken.

God says Gideon, if I allow you to win on your terms then your people will become arrogant. And you will not know the miracle working power of God in you.

Three things you must do in order to win this battle.

1. **Excuse the Cowards** – go whisper in every mans ear if you are scared go home and twenty-two thousand men went home and only ten thousand remained.

My friend, some people you are better off without. Fear is contagious and paralyzing. There are some people who are fearful and if allowed will attempt to talk you out of your victory. Because not only does misery love company, so do cowards.

Everybody you can count you can't count on. The truth is some people will abandon and abort you because they would've wanted the credit. However, when people leave don't mismanage the moment by over internalizing it as rejection, it may be Gods protection.

There will be seasons where you must encourage yourself. The story is told about a man who went to the grocery store one day with his two-year-old toddler. And you know how toddlers can be, very antsy and impatient. As the man pushed the basket down the aisle doing his grocery shopping the little boy kept getting into everything possible. He would knock things off the shelf, scream and cry to get out of the basket sporadically. And the man just kept saying hold on mark it's going to be OK mark. Mark hang in there, you can make it mark. This went on for several minutes the little boy refusing to be quiet. The little boy continued in his mischievous unintentional way. However the man kept saying verbally it's OK mark we're almost finished hang on in there mark we're almost done mark. When the gentleman got up to the register the cashier looked at him and said Sir I want to commend you on how you handled little mark. The gentleman looks at the cashier and says ma'am his name is John my name is mark. What he was saying was I was encouraging myself. And there are times when you must excuse the cowards.

Sometime some people had to leave and fall off and let us down because they would've wanted the credit, but God wants the glory out of our story.

Secondly if you want to win the battle there will be times you have to:

2. ***Exclude the careless-*** Notice he says to Gideon you still have too many. Lead them down to the water and I will try them for you. So, he says to Gideon everyone that lapped like a dog out of their hands are who you shall set aside and it was 300 who lapped like a dog out of their hands and the others bowed down and drank sticking their heads down to the water. God said I'll try them for you. Sometimes if you get out of God's way the trash will take itself out.

We learn from this who the careless are. You see those that brough water up and lapped like a dog out of their hands were knowledgeable enough to know if you bring the water up to your mouth, you can still be alert and aware of your surroundings and not get ambushed. Those that stuck their mouths in the water were careless and had no defense. When you get rid of careless people you soon realize. Everybody in your crowd isn't in your corner.

Now that we have eliminate the scared, we need to begin with those who are skilled

Some folks are more trouble than they are worth. Stop trying to give giraffe vision to turtle level vision people. Kindergarten minded Christians can't handle college level ideas.

There was a citywide Black out in New York City in 1977. But someone couldn't help but notice the statue of liberty was still lit up. They discovered it got its power from another source because it was powered by New Jersey.

Lastly after you have excused the cowards, and excluded the careless, its then time to

3. *Enlist the committed-* committed people are the people who are left when everyone else has had a chance to leave and go home.

So, God says to Gideon trust me. And if you have ever had any dealings with God, you know his track record is on his resume.

The same God that stepped out into nowhere looked out into nothing and said let there be and created this global ball called planet earth. He hung the sun as the golden medallion across the neck of the sky so that the moon could primp at night. He made lunar looking glass out of the moon and gave incandescence to the stars. He's the same God that gave the kaleidoscopic colors to the rainbow. The same God that gave liquidity to water and viscosity to oil. He gave roof roof to the dog and meow to the cat, a wiggle to the worm, a sense of humor to the hyena and an attitude to the alligator. If he can do all of that the certainly, he can give Gideon the battle with 300 men.

Well now we are down to the finale, now we are down to where the rubber meets the road and to some it may still seem a little scary, a little overwhelming, So God says his track record is on his resume God's resume. So, God gives Gideon a scary, skilled, and strategic vison.

Break the pitchers. Which were these lanterns that once you broke them open the light could shine through. Sometimes the greatest light comes through the most broken vessels. Then God says to Gideon break your men up and send the 300 men in quadrants to opposite sides of the tops of the valleys. Then tell them to follow your lead and what they see you do, follow suit. And after they break the pictures and their lights shined, they were told to blow their trumpets! Wait a minute I thought we were going to war, not choir rehearsal. Yet the implication is this that when their enemy saw all of the light from every direction on top of the valley and heard the trumpets noise coming from multiple directions the enemy got confused and started killing each other and they felt like they were trapped and outnumbered because of the effects of the light and noise and the element of surprise. In retrospect Gideons army was not made up of militaristic trained soldiers, but rather he had a rag tag crew of farmers and willing men who did need military training they needed to know how to follow instructions and be coachable. God did the rest. I'm reminded of a song that says.

Have you any river that seems uncrossable?

Have you any mountain that you cannot tunnel through?

God specializes in things that seem impossible and He can do what no other Power can do!

Another song writer chimed in and said, "Tell me who can stand before us when call on that great name!"

The fight is fixed because all you need is God and a Slim Chance.

The story is told of a young man who was reared in a solid God-fearing family. He turned 18 and was about to go out on his own. Before he moved out, he went to his mother and father to get some advice. His father said son when you go out on your own, I want you to remember 3 things and these 3 things will take you through your life successfully. His father said we want you to learn how to lie, beg, and steal. The young man was devastated, he asked his father why he would give him this horrible advice, when all his life they had trained him to do the right things and have moral rectitude. His father said, "Son you don't understand. We want you to learn how to lie at the feet of Jesus because at the feet of Jesus love abides. Then we want you to learn how to beg him for a little more mercy because on this journey you're going to have to beg him for more mercy, because our faults are multiplied daily. But then when life gets you down and you can't see a way out of the storm, just still away and fall on your knees and tell God that you can't make this journey without him. In other words, learn how to lie beg and steal.

Getting ISH Done

ALL IN: Looking For Donkeys - Finding My DESTINY!

1Samuel 9:1-20 (AMP)
¹ THERE WAS a man of Benjamin whose name was Kish son of Abiel, the son of Zeror, the son of Becorath, the son of Aphiah, a Benjamite, a mighty man of wealth and valor.

² Kish had a son named Saul, a choice young man and handsome; among all the Israelites there was not a man more handsome than he. He was a head taller than any of the people.

³ The donkeys of Kish, Saul's father, were lost. Kish said to Saul, Take a servant with you and go, look for the donkeys.

⁴ And they passed through the hill country of Ephraim and the land of Shalishah, but did not find them. Then they went through the land of Shaalim and the land of Benjamin, but did not find them.

⁵ And when they came to the land of Zuph, Saul said to his servant, Come, let us return, lest my father stop worrying about the donkeys and become concerned about us.

⁶ The servant said to him, Behold now, there is in this city a man of God, a man held in honor; all that he says surely comes true. Now let us go there. Perhaps he can show us where we should go.

⁷ Then Saul said to his servant, But if we go, what shall we bring the man? The bread in our sacks is gone, and there is no gift for the man of God. What have we?

⁸ *The servant replied, I have here a quarter of a shekel of silver. I will give that to the man of God to tell us our way-*

⁹ *(Formerly in Israel, when a man went to inquire of God, he said, Come, let us go to the seer, for he that is now called a prophet was formerly called a seer.)*

¹⁰ *Saul said to his servant, Well said; come, let us go. So they went to the city where the man of God was.*

¹¹ *As they went up the hill to the city, they met young maidens going out to draw water, and said to them, Is the seer here?*

¹² *They answered, He is; behold, he is just beyond you. Hurry, for he came today to the city because the people have a sacrifice today on the high place.*

¹³ *As you enter the city, you will find him before he goes up to the high place to eat. The people will not eat until he comes to ask the blessing on the sacrifice. Afterward, those who are invited eat. So go on up, for about now you will find him.*

¹⁴ *So they went up to the city, and as they were entering, behold, Samuel came toward them, going up to the high place.*

¹⁵ *Now a day before Saul came, the Lord had revealed to Samuel in his ear,*

¹⁶ *Tomorrow about this time I will send you a man from the land of Benjamin, and you shall anoint him to be leader over My people Israel; and he shall save them out of the hand of the Philistines. For I have looked upon the distress of My people, because their cry has come to Me.*

¹⁷ *When Samuel saw Saul, the Lord told him, There is the man of whom I told you. He shall have authority over My people.*

[18] Then Saul came near to Samuel in the gate and said, Tell me where is the seer's house?

[19] Samuel answered Saul, I am the seer. Go up before me to the high place, for you shall eat with me today, and tomorrow I will let you go and will tell you all that is on your mind.

[20] As for your donkeys that were lost three days ago, do not be thinking about them, for they are found. And for whom are all the desirable things of Israel? Are they not for you and for all your father's house?

ALL In: Looking for Donkeys and Finding your Destiny. My brothers and sisters our text this morning in a nutshell is about a young Old Testament character by the name of Saul who is about to be the newly inaugurated King of Israel. Now understand that although David was Gods Choice, Saul would be king out of necessity, because in previous verses in this Old Testament narrative Israel Gods people went to the prophet Samuel who had set his sons up as judges over Israel and the people said to Samuel your sons aren't like you. Make us a king like all the other nations, and this grieved the prophet's heart. He went to God and was travailing, and God said they are not rejecting you they are reject me. l will give them a king. and Saul is chosen for the assignment. But was not ready yet and God had to get the word to him about his destiny. He is a young man when we find him in first Samuel, he is a young man with an assignment on his life with a call on his life. However sometimes whenever God has a call on your life when God has an anointing on your life, he must get you away from those who are too familiar with you. Because sometimes when people know us, when they are related to us, or when they have too much access to us. They only want to relegate you to what they know of you and what they knew of you, and they don't have the ability in many cases to speak to who you will become.

Therefore, God must separate you, because when people don't have a proper revelation of who you are they miss handle, mistreat, abuse and misuse what God has deposited in you. When people don't have the proper revelation of who you are they always want to speak to where you were and not to where you are going and if you are surrounded by people who have no regard for what God is doing in your life you will have people around you who will keep you with a fat history but you will have a malnourished future. God must separate you to get you around somebody who can speak to you in terms of the level that God is taking you. My daughter Brianna taught me a term when she graduated from Vanderbilt law school, she taught me something in court when the judge walks in everyone stands. Not necessarily because of the man or the woman who sit in the seat of judge, but for the office that they represent. They sit higher normally than everyone else in the courtroom because in Latin there is a term that translates as familiarity breeds contempt meaning they want to set a precedence that there is a difference between the judge and everyone else. You have to ask for permission to approach the judge, you have to have a representative or an attorney to speak on your behalf. And you only speak to the judge when spoken too, because familiarity breeds contempt meaning that the more familiar you are the more relaxed you are the more common you are with the people a level of respect can be lost or they tend to lose respect. Therefore there are boundaries to make sure no one diminishes the honor that comes along with the judge likewise in our lives the closer people are to us the closer you allow people to get the respect diminishes and pretty soon they get too comfortable and too common with you and they treat you like a regular Joe so God has to allow some people to fall away from you .... it's not that you are better it's not that you are acting funny it's not that you've changed as much as it is you need to be in the company of some people who have a regard and a respect for all that God has placed in you.

And God will use certain circumstances certain incidents two force you into another location and atmosphere where he has someone who can speak to your future and not just constantly bring up your past. There's always a group of people they want to talk about the old you and I remember when and I knew them when but the truth of the matter is I need some people who can speak to the future me even when I'm not my best self they still can see the prophetic potential, they still got a feeling that there is more to you than meets the eye because you are Destiny's Child and God will sometimes use a problem to get you to your purpose.

Yes, my brothers and sisters when you make a decision to be all in with God, he'll use predicaments he'll use circumstance he'll use your mistakes your missteps your fault your flaws your failures your potential your promise your gifts your talents he'll use at all to get you to destiny.

But there are some seasons that aren't designed to get you ready for your destined place and God uses those situations and those seasons and those storms and those trials and those broken days and those tear-stained eyes days and those depressed days and those see nothing days to maneuver you to be in position to hear a word from the Lord. God never wastes a storm he never wastes pain. He uses it all because destiny is over your life and you can't die early because He started something in you and he will accomplish what he set out to do.

Dreams don't come with expiration dates.

I admonish somebody in 2024 stop cursing your past stop calling everything that happened to you a mistake for if you learn from it: it's not a mistake it's experience and now it's on the resume of your life. and you don't have to be ashamed of it because now you know what you did not know before you went through what you had to go through. now you got a story to tell now you got a testimony. That if it had not been for the Lord on your side we wouldn't have made it we had some breakdowns, but we also had some breakthroughs now I can appreciate the Valley now I can appreciate the lessons and the blessings. now I really know what I'm made of.

Bible says that God had to get Saul away from his family and from his kinfolk from his home to get him to somebody that could speak to his life on another level.

The text in a nutshell says that His fathers donkeys were lost, somebody shout the donkeys or lost what my brothers and sisters the text is tailored to teach us today that on your way to destiny you're gonna go through several seasons.

On your way to destiny you gonna have Some issues but you cannot quit you cannot give up on who you are in God.

God carries us through somethings on our way to destiny so that when you get to destiny It won't mess you up and you won't mess it up. and the Bible says that God used this situation of the donkeys being lost Get him to his destiny and sometimes you gotta realize it will be a problem that leads you to your purpose.

In 1981 a writer in Hollywood came up with an idea for a show pilot for young actors and actresses who were coming to los angeles and Hollywood area looking t for their big break, but many he noticed lacked experience they were talented and gifted but they were diamonds in the rough, they needed to be developed and so he comes up with a great idea called not quiet ready for prime time television. And it would be aired late at night where the viewership was low because its easier to mess up in front of 300,000 people than it is to mess up in front of 30 million so they put it on late on Saturday night and it was so that these young future budding stars who were young and inexperienced could work on memorizing lines and work on staying in character and holding a straight face and knowing when to show emotion and how to morph into a character and make a character come alive and learn how to ablib and improvise etc...

But the network was not interested in something with such a weird title like not quite ready for primetime television. So, it was changed to Saturday night live and it spawned some of Hollywood's biggest names like Eddie Murphy and John Belushi and Steve Martin and the list goes on. But we would have never known who they were if it were not for someone recognizing that they had a gift, but their skills needed to be honed and they needed a chance to work through some stuff. Yes, they were talented but they weren't quite ready for prime time television and Saturday night live end up becoming one of the highest rated and watch shows all over the world with the highest Neilson Ratings in television history but really it was an incubator for raw talent that wasn't quite ready for prime time but this was to get them ready for prime time.

And I say to somebody watching me right now... don't become weary in well doing it may seem like you are in the shadows and it may seem like others careers or businesses or ideas took off before yours ...but trust me Wherever God has you right now working in seemingly anonymity or obscurity GOD KNOWS WHERE YOU ARE WHO YOU ARE AND WHAT YOU ARE CAPABLE OF AND ALL THOUGH YOU MAY NOT HAVE ARRIVED TO THE MAIN STAGE WORK AS THOUGH YOU ARE DOING IT UNTO THE LORD BECAUSE ALL IT IS GOD IS GETTING YOU READY FOR PRIMETIME...I DON'T KNOW WHY HE TAKES US THE ROUTE HE DOES I DON'T KNOW WHY HE DOES IT THE WAY HE DOES IT ALL I KNOW IS IM NOT GONE BE COMPLAINING ABOUT WHAT GOD IS DOING FOR THE PASTOR UP THE STREET IM GONE KEEP ON ROCKING AND DOING MY THANG HE HAS ASSIGNED ME TO DO AT MOUNT PLEASANT BECAUSE QUIET AS IT IS KEPT I

BELIEVE GOD IS GETTING ME READY FOR PRIME TIME CAN SOMEBODY SHOUT GOD IS GETTING ME READY FOR PRIME TIME ....THATS WHERE WE FIND SAUL ...

The Bible says Bible says his father instructed him to get a servant to go with him to go look for the donkeys, the bible refers to them as she asses which were the transportation of that day. They went and passed through several places my brothers and sisters I come by here to serve notice ...That because you are Destiny's Child God has not forgotten your address God is not angry with you God is not up in heaven playing games with you. You heard me teach on several occasions that God's name is Jehovah Jireh a it means God is a provider pro means ahead vide is where we get the word video which means to see it literally means God has already seen ahead So what may shock you never surprises God. nothing catches God off guard nothing sneaks up on God realize that God is carrying you through certain seasons so you got to stop saying I'm going through and start saying I'm growing through you got to understand my brothers and sisters that life is like an elevator and on your way to the top you may have to stop In let some folks off especially when you get to a place where good enough is not enough, and you realize that there's more to you then meets the eye somebody type on the screen an shout at the same time I've got destiny on my mind.

Saul was connected to the servant and you gotta have the right people around you you gotta learn how to do your proper research before you allow people into very secret and sacred places in your life. For some people only want to ambush your desire for more because they fear you graduating and leaving them behind so they want to relegate you to success that they can manage.

And I challenge you to surround yourself with people who are not secretly hoping you fail. Saul had a servant who cared just as much about finding the donkeys as he did because the servant understood that his destiny and success was tied to Sauls success.

Oh, how I long and pray for members who would tap into what God is doing in my life. I often wonder with all the word that you've heard me preach why or when are some of you gonna tap into all the resources god has given you in your pastor. You have a pastor who is an an and a Presario and a investor and a dreamer so why are you living defeated ...shame on you if you getting this level of word but you still living beneath your privilege.

And by the time we find Saul and his servant searching for Saul's father kish's donkeys they went through four areas and regions all to no avail and they could not seem to find the lost donkeys and when they were about to give up. The servant said Saul please I sense that we are too close to give up and quit. and God sent me here on a divine assignment SO I came by here to serve notice that on your way to Destiny I don't care how life beat you down look at somebody and tell them you can quit now.

I double dog dare you type it in the comments shout it in your living room or wherever you are shout it loud I can't quit now.

Because destiny is waiting on you just around the next corner and if you abort the mission early if you quit now, you'll never know what could have been if you would just have pressed your way through this next season because you got destiny on your mind you are Destiny's Child. The Bible says they went through four main areas in particular its right there in the Bible if you haven't tore it out, The Bible says they went through Mount Ephraim means fruitfulness because sometimes when you're on your way to destiny you're going to go through some seasons that seem fruitful they seem promising and seem like yeah that's the one you seem like you have found the one yeah but guess what you got to go through those seasons that appear to be fruitful because God has to raise your confidence to a level to understand that you can rise above mediocrity. It looks like a good relationship. It seems like it's a good fit and then it fizzles out or it was fruitful and now its fruitless. But you had to go through it. So, you would learn how to stop trying to force stuff that doesn't fit. So, you can't settle for the first thing smoking… don't settle for the first somebody come along and buy you a ham sandwich and a frosty and now yall moving in together no I need to see how long it will prove fruitful, because salt looks like sugar but it sure isn't sweet it.

And then they went through the Bible says they went through shalisha shalisha means 3rd third row intensification it means when you try some over and repeatedly seem like it doesn't work but you got to understand sometimes God will give you successful failure. He'll let you pick it up and then he will let it break down because if he lets you do it in your own confidence, you'll break your arm patting yourself on the back talking about look what I did, so God must give you some successful failures so that we'll understand you can't do it by yourself. but to learn the lesson you had to retake the test because you didn't get it that first time and it's ok because you don't always get it on the 1st or 2nd go around. Sometimes the 3rd is a charm or it could be harmful but don't stop trying. Life is not like school. Because in school they teach you the lesson and then give you the test, but God will give you the test and then teach you the lesson.

The Bible says they went through shaleem did they went to shaleem means dusk it means when you're right on the edge of a breakthrough when you're so close you can taste it. Sometimes the darkest hour really is right before daybreak or dawn.

Then they go through the tribe of the Benjamite's and Saul was from there and he was of the tribe of Benjamin but you got to understand sometimes You must go through some stuff that your family can't bail you out of that your family can't get you out of that your family can't save you because if you're family saves you or comes to your rescue then they will want the credit. So, God will let you get around strangers and sometimes they will be a bigger blessing than family because if your family does it, they want the credit. And they can't wait normally to hold it over your head. I've learned it's not the length of the relationship, but it's the strength of the relationship. Eventually they go through Zuph which means honey or sweet spot. Yet to no avail. And they run into some shepherd girls, who are watering their flocks, and they ask them, have they seen the Seer? In biblical days sometimes the prophet was called a seer. They responded oh he doesn't come down here, he is up in the high place. In other words, they were telling Saul and his servant that they were looking too low. They needed to elevate their vision. Many times, we don't achieve great things because of low expectations. We must think higher and bigger when Destiny is on the horizon. Think Higher!

Pastor Joel Osteen in his book your best life now, tells the story of a young attorney who was a new Junior partner at a firm. The powers that be attempting to see if he was worth his salt, assigned him a case that was difficult to say the least, also couple that with the fact that it was for an Arabian King so there was so much political tape involved. The young attorney surprisingly found some information that moved the judge to rule in favor of the Sheik and therefore he won the case for the client. He received a call the next week from the Sheik sharing with the atty. That it was the custom in his country, that when someone did something of this magnitude for a person the custom is they would reward the person with a gift. The attorney told the sheik because of his firm's policy there was no way he could ethically accept a gift. The Sheik assured him that he had cleared it with the owners of the firm, and he would be insulted if he did not fulfill the custom and so he asked the young attorney again was there anything he needed or wanted or could use. The attorney realizing the Arabian Shiek was not going to give in, finally said yes, I could use a set of golf clubs. The King said great consider it done. A month later the young attorney received a FedEx Certified package that he had to sign for. He opened the large envelop and inside was two free and clear titles in his name for two of the largest, most exclusive golf courses in the state. The attorney thought obviously this was a mistake so he called the title company to see if they had made an error and he was willing to do what it took to correct this obvious mistake. The title company, however, confirmed that the titles in his name were not a mistake and he had full ownership and authority over the golf courses. He found out who was behind the deal, and it was the wealthy Arabian King. He called the sheik to find out if he mistakenly signed them over by accident, and the sheik replied you said you could use a set of golf clubs, so I purchased the best two I could find. The problem was the attorney was thinking in terms of Golf clubs, for instance like a five iron and a putter etc. Yet the sheik thought in terms of clubs being courses. And his wealth knew no limits, so the cost of the golf courses was pennies compared to his wealth. My point is when it comes to God, he thinks in terms of courses, so we need to stop asking for clubs. The bible says in *Isaiah 55:8-9 (CEV):*

[8] The LORD says: "My thoughts and my ways are not like yours. [9] Just as the heavens are higher than the earth, my thoughts and my ways are higher than yours.

The passage ends beautifully with Saul and his servant going up to the high place. They meet Samuel and he declares to them that he knows who they are and why they are there. However, they weren't there as they assumed to get insight on finding the donkeys, as a matter of fact he told them to rest their minds the donkeys had been found 3 days ago. Yet they were there so they could meet him, and he could tell Saul about how he was destined to be the king over Israel because it was his destiny.

Had it not been for lost donkeys he wouldn't have found his destiny. It blows my mind that all the places life will take you are just pieces in your puzzle to get you to destiny. You are Destiny's Child.

Stay Tuned and Watch This Spot.

www.CharlesBond.com

www.TheRealCharlesBond.com

TheRealCharlesBond@gmail.com

The I'm @ Peace T-shirt Line, The Shalom Candle Line and other merch is available on the Charlebond.com website.

**Stay Tuned Peace U!
Peace University coming soon!**

Getting ISH Done